THE
POLITICALLY
CORRECT
COOKBOOK

A KITCHEN GUIDE FOR THE 90'S

By
CATHERINE DANIEL VONDERAHE

WHITE PINES PRESS

P. O. BOX 472
GROVEPORT, OHIO 43125

With sincere thanks to my family and friends for their loving support and encouragement.

THE POLITICALLY CORRECT COOKBOOK
A KITCHEN GUIDE FOR THE 90's

Copyright © 1993 by Catherine Daniel Vonderahe.
All Rights Reserved.

ISBN 0-9640290-0-6

Front and back cover illustrations by Shawn Porter.
Illustrations on pages 10, 11, 20, 21, 25, 31, 35, 37, 50, 54, 72, 75, 77, 94, 100, 102, 105, 109, and 118 by Shawn Porter.

Graphic design by Solunar Graphics, Columbus, Ohio.

*"Man does not live by words alone,
despite the fact that sometimes
he has to eat them."*

—Adlai Stevenson

A note from the author:

This book is a work of fiction. The names used herein are those of public figures. None of these persons has actually contributed to this book, nor have they endorsed any of these recipes.

The dishes described in this culinary work are meant to be served with a grain of salt and consumed with the tongue planted firmly in the cheek.

6/17/97   **Bon Apetit!**

Rick,
Because laughter
is the best medecine —
Keep on Cookin'!
gee fee.
Catherine Vondell

INTRODUCTION

The 1990's is truly the era of "Political Correctness" in America. Our language, our symbols, our clothing, our relationships are all being redefined according to a new code of acceptability. Political Correctness seeks to accept everyone and offend no one.

We refer to "alternate lifestyle choices," "economically challenged persons," "environmentally friendly industries." We wear shoes and clothing which contain no animal skins or furs. We wash our hair with shampoos that have been tested only on humans. We reuse and recycle everything from milk cartons to newspapers to spouses.

And nowhere is Political Correctness more alive than in our nation's capitol. Our courts, cabinets, and legislators debate the correctness of America's military, its schools, its corporations and the very lives of its citizens!

And so it is to the kitchens and dining rooms of the Washington Elite that we turn for inspiration for this Culinary Guide for the 90's —

THE POLITICALLY CORRECT COOKBOOK!

TEST YOUR POLITICAL CORRECTNESS QUOTIENT

Throughout the book you will find questions to test your *Political Correctness Quotient* or *PCQ*. Use these questions while you are awaiting the next step in a recipe; and, at the same time, increase your knowledge and correctness quotient!

The answers to the *PCQ* questions can be found at the back of the book following the index. It is okay to cheat, but be careful! *GETTING CAUGHT* is definitely <u>not</u> Politically Correct!

Scoring your Political Correctness Quotient

Give yourself one point for each question, or part of a question, which you answered correctly. Add up your total points and refer to the key below.

Score 0 to 20: Hopelessly incorrect! Go back to your cave and wait until Nixon runs again!

Score 21 to 50: Moderately correct, there may be hope.

Score 51 to 70: Enviably correct, submit your resumé for one of the many unfilled Clinton Administration appointments.

Score 71 and up: Perfectly correct! You must already work in Washington. *YOU* write the next book!

CONTENTS

The 1992 presidential campaign was a hard-fought battle, pitting the young Democratic Governor from Little Rock against a G.O.P. in the White House, and spiced by the on-again, off-again candidacy of a Texas billionaire.

The American people were subjected to endless hours of televised campaign coverage. The "Spin Doctors" feverishly turned the images, packaging the candidate to sell to the voters. Staged Town Meetings, Formal Debates, Chart-Chats, Info-mercials, and True-Confessions Sessions filled the airwaves.

Candidates traversed the land via bus tours and train tours, shaking hands and kissing babies from sea to shining sea. Promises dripped, like honey, from the smiling candidates' lips, feeding the hungry masses at countless rallies.

When the early November sun had set on the last polling places in the West, the people had "Voted for Change." A "New Covenant" was made and a "New Kind of Democrat" was headed for Washington.

CHAPTER ONE
ON THE
CAMPAIGN TRAIL

DUCK THE ISSUES

CAMPAIGN TRAIL BALONEY

BILL AND AL'S BUS-STOP BARBECUE

MOCK APPLE PIE

SOAK THE RICH!

CHAMPAIGN PROMISES

FUDGE THE FACTS

MIDDLE CLASS TAX CUT

HARD TIMES CASSEROLE

MUD-SLINGERS' PIE

FLIP-FLOP FLAPJACKS

JAMES CARVILLE'S GARNISHING TRUTHS

DAN QUAYLE'S ALL-AMERICAN P-O-T-A-T-0-E SALAD

H. ROSS PEROT'S TEXAS SHORTCAKES

ADMIRAL JAMES STOCKDALE'S BANANAS SLIP

★ ★

DUCK THE ISSUES

Careful preparation and handling
are important to avoid the grease
and get to the meat!

1 duck, cleaned
1 jar currant jelly
2 cups orange juice

In a small bowl, combine jelly and orange juice. Quarter duck; place in roaster. Roast at 400°F for 1 hour, basting often with jelly and orange juice mixture.

CAMPAIGN TRAIL
BALONEY

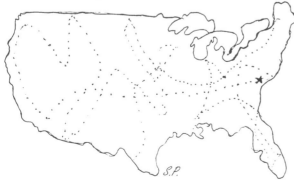

Good baloney is the
mainstay of all
political campaigns!

½ cup sharp Cheddar cheese
2 tblsp. pickle relish
1 tblsp. grated onion
1 tsp. prepared mustard

Combine all ingredients. Stir well until blended. Use as a spread for crackers or sandwiches.

BILL AND AL'S BUS STOP BARBECUE

Travelling the country by bus allows a sampling of great all-American fare.

8 franks split lengthwise
1 tbls. flour
¾ cup water
½ cup catsup
2 tbls. vinegar
2 tsp. sugar
1 tsp. prepared mustard

Place franks in frying pan. Blend flour and 2 table-spoons of the water in a small bowl; add remaining ingredients, mix well. Pour over the franks. Simmer 30 minutes. Multiplying all ingredients by 50 offers an economical way to feed the masses at a bus stop rally.

MOCK APPLE PIE

"...vote for me and I'll give you family values."

Bill Clinton

3 egg whites
1 cup sugar
20 all purpose crackers, crushed
½ teaspoon baking powder
½ teaspoon vanilla
1 cup nuts, chopped
Whipped cream

Beat egg whites until stiff, then gradually add sugar and vanilla while beating. Mix baking powder with crushed crackers; add to egg whites. Fold in chopped nuts. Pour into lightly buttered pie plate. Bake at 350° for 30 minutes. To serve, garnish with whipped cream, tell 'em it's apple — they fall for it every time.

★ ★

SOAK THE RICH!

Enjoy this sumptuous dessert now,
you'll pay for it later!

1 box Devil's Food cake mix
1½ pounds sweet cherries
3 eggs
⅓ cup vegetable oil
1⅓ cups water
Sugar
Kirsch liqueur
6 ounces semisweet chocolate chips
2 cups heavy cream
1 sweet chocolate bar, grated

P.C.Q. #1

Which of the following was not a Clinton campaign promise?

a) I will reverse the policy banning homosexuals from serving in the Armed Forces.
b) I will develop a National Healthcare System within the first 60 days of my administration.
c) I will not raise taxes on the middle class to pay for my programs.
d) I will keep a Kosher kitchen in the White House.
e) I will have a cabinet that looks like America.
f) After I am elected I will not subject the American people to anymore news video footage of my jogging.
g) I will appoint my wife to act as co-president.

Grease and flour two 9"x13" baking pans. Prepare cake mix as directed on package; pour batter into prepared pans, dividing evenly. Bake at 350° for 15 minutes, or until cake springs back when lightly touched. Cool in pans for 10 minutes; remove; cool completely on wire racks.

While cakes are baking, pit cherries and remove stems. Cut each cherry in half. Wrap ⅓ of cherries in plastic wrap; refrigerate. In medium bowl, place remaining cherries with ¼ cup Kirsch, let soak for 30 minutes, stirring often.

When cake is cool, drain cherry mixture, reserving syrup. Place one layer on large sterling silver tray. Prick top of both layers with a fork; spoon cherry syrup over both layers.

In small bowl, beat heavy cream with 1 tablespoon of sugar and 1 tablespoon of Kirsch, at medium speed until soft peaks form. Spread a scant cup of whipped cream onto bottom layer of cake. Spoon drained cherry halves onto cream; top with another scant cup of whipped cream; top with remaining layer of cake. Spread top and sides of cake with about 2 cups of whipped cream. Gently press shaved chocolate onto sides of cake. Decorate top of cake with remaining whipped cream, piping a decorative border around the edge. Garnish with refrigerated cherry halves and grated chocolate.

Serve your elitist-snob guests lavish portions on heirloom china; accompany with demitasse of espresso and V.S.O.P. brandy in lead crystal snifters. Delight in the luxury of this dessert while commiserating about the lack of cheap illegal aliens for domestic labor, the demise of mink, and the specter of enormous tax increases.

CHAMPAIGN PROMISES

"I will not raise taxes on the Middle Class to pay for these programs."

Bill Clinton
Presidential Debate East Lansing
October 19, 1992

4 bottles fine, domestic Champagne
4 bottles dry, white wine
4 — 12-ounce cans frozen lemonade
40 ounces carbonated water
Ice ring with maraschino cherries
    and lemon slices

Combine champagne, white wine, lemonade and soda in a large punch bowl. Gently float ice ring in center. Serves 50.

After the first couple of glasses, when the crowd is feeling good, you can switch to the really cheap stuff — no one will ever know the difference.

FUDGE THE FACTS

A little fudge here, a little fudge there...

4½ cups sugar
Pinch of salt
2 tablespoons butter
12 ounces semisweet chocolate chips
1 tall can evaporated milk
12 ounces sweet German chocolate
1 pint marshmallow cream
2 cups chopped nuts

Boil sugar, salt, butter and milk for 6 minutes. Place remaining ingredients in a large bowl. Pour hot sugar and milk mixture over all. Beat until chocolate is melted. Pour into buttered pan. Let stand for several hours before cutting. Cut into small squares and store in an airtight container. Makes 2 pounds.

MIDDLE CLASS TAX CUT

A *choice cut, artfully prepared and masterfully presented!*

"Middle-class taxpayers will have a choice between a children's tax credit or a significant reduction in their income tax rate."
— *Bill Clinton*
<u>*Putting People First*</u>

EDITOR'S NOTE:
We are sorry that this recipe is unavailable. As of the date of this printing, the *"Middle Class Tax Cut"* was nowhere to be found.

Suggested Substitution:
"Tax and Spend Souffle," Chapter 4, page 78.

P.C.Q. #2
Seek and Find

Circle the following list of words in the block of letters below. The words may be written across, up and down, or diagonally and may be spelled forwards or backwards. The secret message will appear when you have circled all of the hidden words.

ELECT	GOT	TAX	SHAFT	SOCKS
NEVER	RAISE	BUCKS	MONEY	SPEND

```
A B L J G S C L P D O S V O M T N H A N K V
M O N E Y L D E U I F Q S B W S S Z B T D L
L D E K D R S V L N J P G K B K P P O F A T
D F V T F I G S A E W L L X C H I G M A P X
S T E L A S P E N D C M T U T O A Y X H J C
Q H R R U V T B T H L T B S Z R S U U S K E
```

HARD TIMES CASSEROLE

"It's the Economy, Stupid!"
When the going gets tough,
the tough gets cooked!

2 pounds round steak
3 cubes beef bouillon, crushed
3 tablespoons soy sauce
2 large onions, peeled and sliced
6 large potatoes, peeled and thinly sliced
2 cups water
Salt and pepper

Cut meat into serving-sized pieces; place in large casserole. Sprinkle with bouillon and soy sauce. Place layers of onion rings and potatoes on top, sprinkling with salt and pepper as you go. Add enough water to fill halfway. Cover and bake at 350° for 2½ hours.

While this is cooking you can check in with the
unemployment office, drop off your grandmother's
silver at the pawn shop, and donate plasma for cash.

P.C.Q. #3

President Clinton's 1992 book
detailing his philosophy of
government is entitled:
a) Bigger Government; Better
   Government
b) Putting People First
c) Making People Pay
d) Making People Poor

MUDSLINGER PIE

Get Down, Get Dirty, <u>Get Even</u>!

30 chocolate sandwich cookies
3 tablespoons butter, melted
1 pint coffee ice cream
2 tablespoons whipped cream
2 tablespoons crème de cocoa
2 tablespoons coffee liqueur
Chocolate syrup topping
Whipped cream for garnish

CRUSH 24 chocolate sandwich cookies finely. **BREAK** the remaining 6 chocolate sandwich cookies into itty, bitty pieces; set aside. Place butter in glass bowl in microwave; **TURN ON THE HEAT** until melted. In a medium sized bowl, mix crushed cookies with melted butter. **PRESS** into 9" pie pan and place in freezer. **WHIP** ice cream with 2 tablespoons whipped cream, the crème de cocoa and coffee liqueur; pour into pie **SHELL**; return to freezer until firm. Drizzle a layer of chocolate topping over frozen pie; **SMEAR** it around until **NOTHING IS LEFT UNCOVERED**. Before serving, **SLAM** on the whipped cream and **SMASH** in some of the reserved cookie pieces. **LOOK OUT!**

FLIP-FLOP FLAPJACKS

*Sure to please everyone,
on all sides of the issues.*

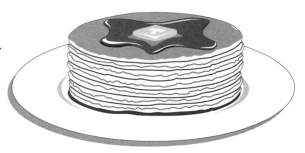

2 cups flour
¼ cup sugar
4 teaspoons baking powder
1 teaspoon salt
2 eggs
1½ cups milk
1 teaspoon vanilla extract
¼ cup vegetable oil
3 cups blueberries

In a large bowl, sift together flour, baking powder and salt. Make a "well" in the center of sifted mixture; crack eggs into "well." Stir until blended. In a small bowl, blend milk, vanilla, and oil; whisk lightly. Pour into flour and egg mixture. Stir to moisten, do not beat batter. Gently fold in blueberries. Pour batter by ¼ cupfuls onto hot griddle. When bubbles appear, flip, cook until lightly browned. Keep warm. Serve with hot maple syrup.

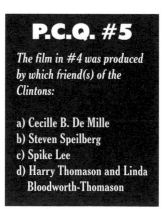

P.C.Q. #4

The film about Bill Clinton which was shown at the 1992 Democratic National Convention was entitled:

a) "The Man from Glad"
b) "The Man from U.N.C.L.E."
c) "The Man from La Mancha"
d) "The Man from Hope"

P.C.Q. #5

The film in #4 was produced by which friend(s) of the Clintons:

a) Cecille B. De Mille
b) Steven Speilberg
c) Spike Lee
d) Harry Thomason and Linda Bloodworth-Thomason

JAMES CARVILLE'S GARNISHING TRUTHS

A slick presentation makes any fare more palatable.

The Radish Rose: Wash radishes, remove leaves and cut off root end. Make cuts in varying depths on all sides of each radish, being careful not to cut through. Place radishes in water and refrigerate for several hours. "Petals" will separate when chilled.

The Cucumber Boat: Cut lengthwise section of cucumber leaving bottom section deeper than the top. Remove seeds and pulp, being careful not to break through skin. Using a sharp paring knife, carefully cut V-shaped notches all around edge to form border. Use to serve dips, spreads, or individual chicken or tuna salads.

The Bread Bowl: Using a serrated knife, cut a small section off the top of a large round loaf of bread. With a small knife, carefully hollow out the inside of the loaf. Fill hollowed-out "boat" with dip and serve with cubes of the bread.

The Green Onion Pom-pom: With a paring knife, slice off the root end of a green onion. Cut off all but 2 inches of the green end. Starting at the top, make slashes down the onion all the way around, leaving about ½ inch uncut at the bottom. Place in ice water and refrigerate to curl the ends. Use to garnish meats, vegetable trays, Mexican dishes and fish.

The Cabbage Bowl: Wash a medium-sized purple cabbage. Cut about ½" off of the core end to allow it to stand flat. Cut about 2" off of the top. With a sharp knife, carefully hollow out cabbage. Place in the center of a large serving tray, fill with dip and surround with fresh crisp vegetables.

Orange Cups: Cut oranges in half. Remove pulp and seeds, use in salads or for juice. Fill orange cups with hot rice and serve around a roast turkey. Use orange cups as containers for individual desserts; sherbet, mousse, or custards.

Just what the spin doctor ordered!

Dan Quayle's All-American P-O-T-A-T-O-E Salad

No matter how you spell it, it tastes great!

2 pounds potatoes (8 to 10 medium)
8 hard-boiled eggs
½ cup celerye, finely chooppped
⅓ cup chopped onione
1¼ cups mayonnaise
1 tablespoon prepared mustarde
1½ teaspoons salte
Pepper to taste
4 sweete pickles, diced
Paprikae to garnish

Washe potatoes; boile in skins until tender; draine and let coole. Peele and dice potatoes. Dice 6 of the boiled eggs; add to potatoes, add celerye, onione and diced sweete pickle. Combine mayonnaise, pickle juice, mustarde, salte and peppere. Folde gently into potatoes, mixing welle. Slice the 2 remaining eggs to garnishe top of potatoe salade. Sprinkle paprikae over all.

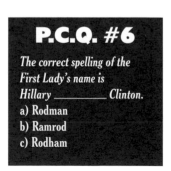

P.C.Q. #6

The correct spelling of the First Lady's name is Hillary _____ Clinton.
a) Rodman
b) Ramrod
c) Rodham

★ ★

S.P.

H. ROSS PEROT'S
TEXAS SHORTCAKE

So simple, Just Fix it and Move On!

2 cups flour, leveled
3 tablespoons sugar
1 heaping teaspoon baking powder
½ cup butter

1 egg, slightly beaten
½ cup milk
1 quart strawberries,
    cleaned, sliced and sugared
Whipped cream

CHART 1

1. Sift flour, sugar and baking powder together.
2. Cut in butter until mixture is crumbly.
3. Stir in egg and milk.

CHART 2

1. Drop by large spoonful onto greased baking sheet.
2. Bake at 425° until golden brown, time will depend on the size of the shortcakes.

CHART 3

1. To serve, split each shortcake; place bottom halves in serving dishes.
2. Ladle strawberries onto cake, place top halves on strawberries.
3. Garnish with plenty of whipped cream and additional strawberries.

What we're gonna do here, ya see, is make some great shortcake. Not one of those pansy, fluffy, lacey-drawers French desserts. I'm talkin' all-American, flag-flyin' stick to your ribs, shortcake. Because you, the owners of the country, asked me to do it. First thing you gotta do is kick the cook outta the kitchen, I'm in charge now. Now check out chart #1. Don't be messin' with me, just do what I say and we can get on with this thing.

Now after you got that going. Excuse me. Can I finish here? I didn't interupt you while you where fixin' your recipe. Now I think that I deserve a little respect here.

Thank you. Now where was I? Oh yeah, chart # 2 Now check this out.

Now listen up here, you people. Don't make 'em too big, or you'll end up with a dough deficit. We've got enough problems with those yo-yo's in Congress using up all of our hard-earned dough! Now, pay attention! I'm not here 'cause I wanna be. You asked me to come here and I think that the least you could do is hear me out on this. Move on to chart # 3. This is important here, ya see? 'Cause if you don't serve 'em right you might as well just throw the whole thing away and have jello. You might just as well shoot yourself in the foot. Cut off your nose, or your ears for that matter, to spite your face. If you don't put this together right the citizens of this country just ain't gonna buy it. You hear me? You're gonna be left with an old dog that won't hunt. A crazy aunt in yer basement. Now get to it!

There now, I told you it would be fine if you'd just do it my way. Now sit down and eat it before it turns to mush!

ADMIRAL JAMES STOCKDALE'S BANANAS SLIP

"Who am I?
Why am I here?"

2 eggs, beaten
2 tablespoons butter
½ cup sugar
1 cup orange juice
2 tablespoons flour
½ cup whipping cream
5 ripe, firm bananas
½ cup chopped peanuts
Whipped cream for garnish

S.P.

In a small saucepan, combine eggs, sugar and orange juice; stir in flour. Cook over medium heat, stirring often until thickened. Remove from heat. Add butter, stir well; chill. When cool, add whipped cream. Slice bananas; in serving bowl, layer bananas and cooled dressing. Top with chopped peanuts. Serve with whipped cream garnish. Refrigerate leftovers. Sweet and Simple!

On January 20, 1993, William Jefferson Blythe Clinton became the 42nd President of the United States. The first "Baby
Boomer" to occupy the White House, Clinton redefines the
image of the presidency. Influenced by Kennedy and Presley,
enamored of fast food and slow jazz, this President adds a new
dimension to the highest office in the land.

With a First Lady who is involved, ambitious and a bit controversial; and an ever-expanding assortment of half-brothers and
would-be half sisters, the first family brings unprecedented diversity to the grand house on Pennsylvania Avenue.

CHAPTER TWO

PRESIDENTIAL FAVORITES

ARKANSAS BUBBA STEW WITH DOWN-HOME CORN FRITTERS
SAIGON SOUP
BILL'S BEST BORSCHT
COMRADE CLINTON'S CLASSIC KIEV
OXFORD ROAST BEEF AND YORKSHIRE PUDDING
RHODES SCHOLAR STEAK AND KIDNEY PIE
HEAVENLY HASH-BROWNS
GENNIFER FLOWERS' CHEESECAKE TARTE
QUICHE AND TELL
BROCCOLI'S BACK!
CHRISTOPHE'S MILLION DOLLAR MOUSSE
NEW-AGED CHEDDAR SQUARES
PRESIDENTIAL PIG-OUT PIZZA
HILLARY'S HONEYDEW-AS-I-SAY SHERBET
THE NEW DEAL DINNER
CHELSEA'S MOVIE-TIME MUNCHIES
"SOCKS" FAVORITE FELINE FEAST
ROCKIN' ROGER'S FUN FLOAT
PUTTIN' ON THE RITZ
DOIN' THYME

ARKANSAS BUBBA STEW

*Squirrel, possum, woodchuck are best,
but you can use store-bought
if yer in the big city!*

1½ pounds stew meat
5 medium potatoes
2 cups carrots, chunked
1 cup chopped onion
1 cup celery, chunked
1 clove garlic, minced

2 cans stewed tomatoes
2 tablespoons dry tapioca
1 tablespoon sugar
2 teaspoons salt
⅛ teaspoon pepper

Combine all ingredients in a Dutch oven. Cover and bake at 275° for 5 hours or until meat is tender. Remove from oven and let stand 5 minutes before serving.

DOWN-HOME CORN FRITTERS

1 – 8¾ ounce can whole kernel corn
Milk
1½ cups all-purpose flour
½ teaspoon salt
¼ cup cornmeal
2 teaspoons baking powder
1 beaten egg
Vegetable oil

Drain corn; reserve liquid. Add enough milk to corn liquid to equal 1 cup. In a medium bowl, stir together flour, cornmeal, baking powder, and ½ teaspoon salt. Add corn, milk mixture and egg. Stir until moistened. In a deep kettle, heat vegetable oil. Drop batter by tablespoon into hot oil. Fry several fritters at a time, turning once to brown. Remove from oil; drain on paper towel. Serve warm with maple syrup. Makes 2 dozen.

SAIGON SOUP

Serve Hot — Avoid Drafts!

2 pounds cabbage
2 pounds ground pork
1 bunch green onion leaves, chopped
½ tablespoon garlic salt
½ tablespoon sugar
Soy sauce
Salt
Pepper

Pre-boil cabbage and onion leaves. Remove cabbage; reserve water. Mix the ground pork with garlic salt, sugar, and a few shakes of soy sauce, salt, and pepper. Detach the cabbage leaves and roll them around thumb-sized pieces of the pork mixture. Carefully place these rolls into the boiling cabbage water; boil until pork is fully cooked. Add more water if necessary. Season to taste. Serve with fried rice.

This will never fill you up. So, after dinner secretly sneak out and grab a burger!

P.C.Q. #7

Which of the following was a reason for Bill Clinton avoiding military service in Vietnam?

a) He didn't like the haircuts.
b) He got there late.
c) He disagreed with the policy banning homosexuals from service.
d) It depends on when you asked him.

BILL'S BEST BORSCHT

A satisfying supper after a long protest march.

1 can condensed consomme
1 can condensed cream of chicken soup
1 can beets, strain off ⅓ of the liquid
1 clove garlic, minced
Sour cream
Chopped herbs

Combine condensed soups, beets, and garlic in blender. Blend until smooth. Chill. Serve cold; garnish with a dollop of sour cream and chopped herbs.

★ ★

COMRADE CLINTON'S CLASSIC KIEV

Chill the vodka, gather the comrades and enjoy!

4 boneless, skinless chicken breasts
6 tablespoons butter, slightly softened
3 slices bread, cut in quarters
4 teaspoons chopped chives
8 tablespoons milk

In a small bowl, combine chives and butter with a fork; refrigerate 30 minutes. Roll butter and chives into 4 equal log-shaped pieces, about 2" long; chill in freezer 30 minutes. While butter logs are chilling, flatten chicken breasts between waxed paper, one at a time until they are about ⅓ inch thick. Place bread in food processor or blender and blend until finely crumbed; place in a shallow dish.

Place one "log" of butter at the long edge of each chicken breast; roll tightly, securing with toothpicks. Dip each rolled breast in milk, then coat with bread crumbs. Place in baking dish and bake at 375° for 45 minutes. Cover with foil for the last 10 minutes to keep bread crumbs from burning.

Fluffy rice pilaf, a crisp green salad with fresh beets, and generous rounds of hearty shepherd's bread make this a sumptuous meal for a cold winter's night.

This is a great menu for a Soviet-themed dinner party. Issue ration cards as invitations. Have guests bring a favorite bit of propaganda to read to the group. Make everyone wait in line to get a drink, to use the bathroom, to serve their dinner plate. Crowd a group of twelve around a table meant for four. Make sure that there is no toilet paper in the guest bath and provide only small shavings of hand soap. Sneak out and siphon the fuel out of your guests' cars, make them line up to buy back a gallon of gas to get home. Surely a memorable evening for all!

★★★

RHODES SCHOLAR STEAK AND KIDNEY PIE

An involved, time-consuming dish,
but well worth it.

¾ pound kidney (or calf liver)
2 tablespoons flour
1 teaspoon salt
1 teaspoon pepper
2 pounds steak, cut into bite-sized pieces
4 tablespoons butter
5 small onions, finely chopped
1 tablespoon flour plus 3 tablespoons water
1 cup double-strength beef bouillon
1 bay leaf
1 teaspoon chopped parsley
⅛ teaspoon ground cloves
½ pound mushrooms, sliced and sautéed
1 tablespoon soy sauce
1-crust pastry for top

Mix together flour, salt, and pepper in a shallow dish. Roll kidney and steak pieces in seasoned flour. In a large, heavy pot sauté onions in butter. Add kidney and steak; brown lightly on all sides. Add bouillon, bayleaf, parsley, and cloves. Stir; cover and simmer 1¼ hours until meat is tender. Add mushrooms and soy sauce. Thicken with flour and water mixture.

Grease a deep round baking dish. Add meat mixture and allow to cool. Prepare pastry (or use 1 refrigerated pie pastry). Place pastry over meat, sealing pastry to the edges of the dish. Make several slits in the top to allow steam to escape. Bake at 450° for 8 to 10 minutes. Reduce heat to 375° and bake an additional 15 minutes until pastry is golden brown.

HEAVENLY HASH BROWNS

Do Not Inhale!

2 pounds frozen hash brown potatoes, thawed
½ cup butter, melted
½ cup chopped onion
1 teaspoon salt
½ teaspoon pepper
2 cups milk
1 can cream of chicken soup
2 cups shredded Cheddar cheese
2 cups corn flakes, crushed
½ cup butter, melted

Grease an extra-large glass baking dish. Place thawed potatoes in dish and cover with ½ cup melted butter. Sprinkle with onion, salt and pepper. Combine milk with undiluted soup; pour over potatoes. Sprinkle Cheddar cheese over mixture. Combine crushed corn flakes with ½ cup melted butter; sprinkle over potato mixture. Bake at 350° for 1 hour, or until potatoes are tender.

If dish starts smoking, cover-up immediately!

P.C.Q. #8

President Clinton has been known to enjoy playing:
a) the field
b) left field
c) around
d) the saxophone
e) all of the above

GENNIFER FLOWERS' CHEESECAKE TARTE

Looks glamorous, but Fast and Easy !

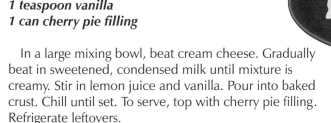

1–9 inch baked pie shell
1–8 ounce package cream cheese
1–14 ounce can sweetened, condensed milk
⅓ cup concentrated lemon juice
1 teaspoon vanilla
1 can cherry pie filling

In a large mixing bowl, beat cream cheese. Gradually beat in sweetened, condensed milk until mixture is creamy. Stir in lemon juice and vanilla. Pour into baked crust. Chill until set. To serve, top with cherry pie filling. Refrigerate leftovers.

QUICHE AND TELL

Too yummy to keep it a secret!

Pie crust mix for two 9-inch pie crusts
2 tablespoons butter, melted
1–10-ounce package frozen, chopped spinach, thawed
¼ pound Swiss cheese, shredded
1 cup half and half
3 eggs
½ teaspoon salt

Grease and flour thirty 1¾-inch muffin pan cups. Prepare pie crust dough as label directs. On lightly floured surface roll pastry dough to ⅛-inch thickness. Cut out 30 circles with a floured, 3-inch round cookie cutter, re-rolling scraps. Line muffin cups with pastry and brush with melted butter. Refrigerate 25 minutes. Drain thawed spinach; place between layers of paper towelling and squeeze to remove water. In a small bowl, mix half and half, eggs and salt; whisk together. Into each pastry circle, place 1 tablespoon of spinach and some shredded cheese. Spoon 1 tablespoon egg mixture into each cup. Bake at 400° for 25 minutes. Serve hot. Makes 30 appetizers.

PRESIDENTIAL HAM AND BROCCOLI ROYALE

You voted for change...
Broccoli's Back!

3 cups cooked rice
2 packages frozen, chopped broccoli
12 tablespoons butter
2 cups fresh breadcrumbs
1 cup chopped onion
6 tablespoons flour
1 teaspoon salt
½ teaspoon pepper
4 cups milk
4 cups cubed ham
1 cup shredded Cheddar cheese

"I do not like broccoli, and I haven't liked it since I was a little kid and my mother made me eat it. And I'm President of the United States and I'm not going to eat any more broccoli."
— *George Bush*

Spoon cooked rice into buttered 4-quart casserole. Arrange broccoli over rice. Melt butter in a small saucepan. Toss 2 teaspoons of melted butter with bread crumbs, set aside. Sauté onions in remaining butter; blend in flour and seasonings. Stir in milk; cook until thick and creamy. Add cubed ham and heat until bubbly; pour over rice and broccoli, layer cheese on top. Sprinkle buttered bread crumbs over all. Bake at 350° for 45 minutes.

CHRISTOPHE'S MILLION DOLLAR MOUSSE

Spare no expense!

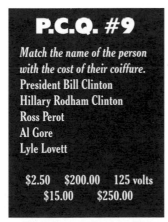

6 ounces rich, sweet chocolate
¼ cup strong, hot coffee
3 egg yolks
1 shot dark rum
3 egg whites
8 ounces whipping cream

Grate chocolate. Place grated chocolate in bowl of food processor; add hot coffee and mix well. Add egg yolks, one at a time. Add rum. In a separate bowl, beat egg whites; fold into chocolate mixture. In another bowl, whip the cream; fold into the chocolate mixture. Pour into crystal goblets; chill. To serve, garnish with whipped cream and shaved chocolate.

*Open the champagne; sit back; relax and enjoy —
let the planes wait! This delight deserves to be savoured!*

P.C.Q. #9

*Match the name of the person
with the cost of their coiffure.*
President Bill Clinton
Hillary Rodham Clinton
Ross Perot
Al Gore
Lyle Lovett

$2.50 $200.00   125 volts
     $15.00 $250.00

P.C.Q. #10

Who of the following Hollywood celebrities visited the President and First Lady at the White House during the first 125 days of the Clinton Administration?
a) Billy Crystal
b) Barbra Streisand
c) Sharon Stone
d) Richard Gere
e) Richard Dreyfuss
f) Paul Newman and
   JoAnn Woodward
g) Quincy Jones
h) Sinbad
i) Christopher Reeve
j) John Ritter
k) Sam Waterston
l) Hammer
m) Lindsay Wagner
n) Judy Collins
o) all of the above

NEW-AGED CHEDDAR SQUARES

A favorite of the whole gang at the Hilton Head Retreat!

4 eggs, well-beaten
¼ cup fine, dry bread crumbs
½ teaspoon salt
⅛ teaspoon pepper
½ teaspoon crushed oregano
3-4 drops hot pepper sauce
½ cup onion, finely chopped
1 clove garlic, minced
2 tablespoons butter
2 cups aged Cheddar cheese, grated
2 — 6-ounce jars marinated artichoke hearts, drained and chopped

P.C.Q. #11

Among Bill Clinton's major goals are:
a) promoting world peace
b) seeking inner peace
c) getting a lil' piece
d) all of the above

Combine beaten eggs, bread crumbs, salt, pepper, oregano, and hot pepper sauce. Sauté onion and garlic in butter. Remove from heat, add cheese and artichokes. Add egg mixture; spread in greased 11" x 7 ½" x ½" pan. Bake at 350° for 30 minutes. Cool slightly, cut into squares. Serve warm. Makes 4 dozen appetizers.

PRESIDENTIAL PIG-OUT PIZZA

*Worth the extra 5 miles that
I have to jog to work it off.*

Crust:
2 cups self-rising flour
²⁄₃ cup milk
¼ cup salad oil
2 tablespoons salad oil

Toppings:
½ cup grated Parmesan cheese
1 – 8 ounce can tomato sauce
1 – 1 pound can whole tomatoes, drained and chopped
½ teaspoon salt
1 teaspoon oregano
¼ teaspoon garlic powder
1 pound Italian sausage, browned and crumbled
½ cup fresh, sliced mushrooms
¼ cup each chopped green pepper and chopped onion
½ pound shredded mozzarella cheese

For crust, combine flour, milk and ¼ cup oil in a large bowl. Stir until mixture forms a rough ball. Smooth dough into a ball. Knead dough 12 times. On a lightly floured surface, roll dough into a large circle, place on a greased pizza pan. Turn up crust to make a 1" edge. Brush with 2 tablespoons oil. Bake at 425° for 25 minutes. Remove from oven. Mix together tomato sauce, chopped tomatoes, salt, oregano and garlic powder in a small bowl. Sprinkle grated Parmesan on crust. Spread tomato sauce on top. Layer on remaining toppings in order given. Return to 425° oven for an additional 20 minutes. Remove from oven and slice.

Pop open a 6-pack, turn on a flick and enjoy! Serves 1!

★ ★

HILLARY'S HONEYDEW-AS-I-SAY SHERBET

½ medium sized honeydew melon
2 cups milk
2 envelopes plain gelatin
2 cups water
¾ cup light corn syrup
½ cup sugar
3 tablespoons lemon juice
¾ teaspoon salt
Green food coloring
Sprigs of mint for garnish

Kindly ask your husband to peel melon half; discard rind and seeds. Then **suggest that he** cut melon into bite-sized pieces and place melon chunks into bowl of food processor; add 1 cup of milk; process on low until smooth; set aside.

Instruct your husband to sprinkle gelatin evenly over remaining 1 cup milk in a 3-quart saucepan; let mixture stand 1 minute; **let husband** sit 1 minute. **Watch him like a hawk** as he cooks the mixture over medium heat, stirring often, until gelatin is completely dissolved. **Before he totally screws it up**, have him remove it from heat; stir in melon mixture, water, corn syrup, sugar, lemon juice and salt. **Direct husband** to add green food color a few drops at a time, stirring until a pleasant color is achieved. Then **make him** pour mixture into a 13"x9" baking pan; cover with foil and place in freezer for 3 hours, stirring occasionally. While mixture freezes **husband can** set the table, finish the laundry, prepare the main course, vacuum the dining room, scrub the toilet, set out hand towels for the guests, and take a 10 minute lunch break. After freezing, **order husband** to spoon mixture into a large, chilled bowl. Beat mixture (not husband) at medium speed, until smooth but still icy. **Supervise as husband** returns mixture to the baking pan, covers and lets it freeze until firm, about 3 more hours. **He can** use this time to draw your bath, prepare the appetizer and salad course, bathe and feed the children, and grab a quick shower and shave.

To serve, let sherbet stand at room temperature for 15 minutes. **While husband** is clearing the table, scoop into parfait glasses; garnish with a sprig of fresh mint. Serve with a flourish while **husband starts** washing dishes. Your guests will rave, and only you will know how easy it was! Makes 12 servings.

NEW DEAL DINNER...
A CHICKEN IN EVERY POT

Eleanor Roosevelt, Former First Lady
as told to
Hillary Rodham Clinton, First Lady

2 chicken breasts
4 chicken legs/thighs
1 bay leaf
1 – 18-ounce package frozen egg noodles
1 large carrot, grated
1 cup grated cabbage
1 medium onion, grated
1 medium potato, grated

Simmer chicken in water with bay leaf about 40 minutes, or until tender. Remove chicken and add noodles, (Eleanor says homemade are best) to boiling chicken broth; cook for 20 minutes. Turn off heat. Add grated vegetables; cover and let stand at least 5 minutes. Remove chicken from bone and cut into small pieces. Add to noodles and serve.

A comforting meal when your husband
has had a tough day on The Hill.

P.C.Q. #12

Hillary Rodham Clinton has served on the boards of which of the following corporations?
a) Wal Mart
b) K Mart
c) T.C.B.Y.
d) Y.O.Y.
e) La Farge
f) The Daughters of the American Revolution
g) The Children's Defense Fund

CHELSEA'S MOVIETIME MUNCHIES

It's so cool to have a movie theater in my own house!

15 cups popped corn
½ cup butter
½ teaspoon salt

¼ cup light corn syrup
½ teaspoon baking soda
1 cup firmly packed brown sugar

Preheat oven to 200°. Divide popcorn between 2 ungreased baking pans, 13" x 9" x 2". In a saucepan, heat brown sugar, butter, corn syrup and salt. Cook, stirring occasionally, until mixture just begins to bubble around the edges. Continue cooking over medium heat for 5 minutes. Remove from heat and stir in baking soda until foamy. Pour onto popcorn, stirring until all popcorn is well coated. Bake at 200° for 1 hour, stirring every 15 minutes. Cool, store in an airtight container.

This is tough on the braces, but it sure tastes great!

"SOCKS" FAVORITE FELINE FEAST

I'm the fat-cat now!

2 cups lobster meat
6 tablespoons butter
2 tablespoons flour
⅓ cup sherry
2 egg yolks
2 cups thin cream
½ teaspoon salt
Dash of cayenne pepper

Place egg yolks and cream in double boiler. Add flour, butter, sherry, salt, and cayenne pepper; mix well. Stir in lobster meat. Cook until thick. Sprinkle with a dash of pepper to serve. People like this, too!

ROCKIN' ROGER'S FUN FLOAT

Party!!!!!!!

1 bottle Cola
2 scoops vanilla ice cream

Place ice cream in a frosted mug, slowly pour cola over ice cream. Add a straw, or if you don't have a straw, a rolled-up $100 bill works just fine.

Turn on music videos and get down!

P.C.Q. #13

Who of the following has not claimed to be Bill Clinton's half brother/sister?

a) Henry Leon Ritzenthaler
b) Sharon Elaine Pettijohn
c) Ross Perot
d) Roger Clinton
e) Hillary Rodham Clinton
f) Rush Limbaugh
g) Joey Butafuoco

P.C.Q. #14

George Clinton was:
a) a used car salesman in Hope, Arkansas
b) a recently discovered half-brother to the President
c) the father of our country
d) Vice President to President James Madison

★ ★

PUTTIN' ON THE RITZ

A Down-home old family favorite.

Henry Leon Ritzenthaler, Half Brother to the President

1 – 20-ounce package frozen broccoli, chopped
1 stick butter, melted
1 sleeve all-purpose crackers, crushed
8 ounces American cheese

P.C.Q. #15

Who was Leslie Lynch King?

Place partially thawed chopped broccoli in a buttered baking dish. Pour half of the melted butter over the broccoli. Mix the remaining melted butter with the crushed crackers. Cut the cheese into cubes and place on the broccoli; sprinkle cracker mixture on top. Bake at 350° for 35 minutes.

This is always a big hit at the family reunion. It seems like the old family tree keeps growing bigger all the time. This is one recipe that can easily be doubled or even tripled to make sure there's enough for the whole gang.

DOIN' THYME

Jane Doe: Inmate, Arkansas State Penitentiary Claims to be Half-Sister to the President

8 tablespoons butter
1 loaf French bread
½ teaspoon dried thyme
½ teaspoon garlic powder

Melt butter in a saucepan and add herbs; simmer for 20 minutes. Split French bread lengthwise, generously spread both halves with herbed butter. Put loaf together and wrap in foil. Heat at 200° for 30 minutes or until crisp.

Highlights of Who's Who in the Clinton White House
Note: Subject to change without notice.

President .... William Jefferson Clinton
Vice President .... Albert Gore Jr.
White House Chief of Staff .... Thomas "Mack" McLarty
White House Counsel .... Bernard Nussbaum
Special Advisor to the President .... David Gergen
Senior Advisor .... George Stephanopolous
White House Press Secretary .... Dee Dee Meyers
U.S. Surgeon General .... Dr. Joycelyn Elders
Health Care Task Force Chief .... Hillary Rodham Clinton
Special Advisor for Health Care .... Ira Magaziner
Department of Agriculture .... The Honorable Mike Espy
Department of Commerce .... The Honorable Ronald H. Brown
Department of Defense .... The Honorable Bobby Inman
Department of Education .... The Honorable Richard W. Riley
Department of Energy .... The Honorable Hazel R. O'Leary
Dept. Health & Human Services .... The Honorable Donna E. Shalala
Dept. of Housing & Urban Development .... The Honorable Henry G. Cisneros
Department of the Interior .... The Honorable Bruce Babbitt
Department of Justice .... The Honorable Janet Reno
Department of Labor .... The Honorable Robert B. Reisch
Office of Management and Budget .... The Honorable Leon E. Panetta
Department of State .... The Honorable Warren M. Christopher
United States Trade Representative .... Ambassador Mickcy Kantor
Department of Transportation .... The Honorable Federico F. Pena
Department of the Treasury .... The Honorable Lloyd Bentsen
Department of Veterans Affairs .... The Honorable Jesse Brown

During the 1992 Presidential Campaign, Bill Clinton promised that if elected, he would appoint a cabinet which "looks like America." The Clinton Cabinet reflects the diversity of our land with Hispanics, African Americans, and women well represented. Clinton broke new Presidential ground by giving major administrative responsibilities to his wife, charging her with heading the Health Care Task Force. Also on the Clinton team are old line party faithfuls, career diplomats, and even a former Reagan White House Advisor!

CHAPTER THREE
THE KITCHEN CABINET

DAVID GERGEN'S EGGS BENEDICT ARNOLD
MCLARTY'S "MIGHTY MACK"
GEORGE'S STEPHANOKOPITA
WEEKENDS AT BERNIE'S
WHITE-HOUSE-LEEKS SOUP!
DEE DEE MEYERS' MEDIA BLINTZES
HILLARY'S HEALTH-NUT COOKIES
IRA MAGAZINER'S HEALTH SHAKE-UP
SURGEON GENERAL'S WEINER-WRAPS AND CONDOMENTS
WARREN CHRISTOPHER'S PROTOCOLIFLOWER SOUP
BUREAU OF ATF TIPS FOR GRILLING
JANET RENO'S TEXAS BARBEQUE
FBI'S MOST WANTED: MACE COOKIES
DEA'S SCRAMBLED BRAINS AND EGGS
CISNEROS' RELLANOS
RON BROWN'S HIGH-LIVERS' PATE
ROBERT'S REISCH PUDDING
WHO'S MINDING THE MINTS?
RICHARD RILEY'S PUBLIC-SCHOOL-LUNCH LOAF
DONNA SHALALA'S PASTA PRIMA-DONNA
LEON PANETTA'S HI-RISE CAKE WITH NO-TRICKLE-DOWN FROSTING
F.E.M.A. FAVORITE: TORNADOES DE BOEUF
D.O.T.'S ROCKY ROAD CAKE

★★★★★★★★★★★★★★★★★★★★★★★★★★★★★★★

DAVID GERGEN'S
EGGS BENEDICT-ARNOLD

6 eggs, poached
3 English muffins, split
6 slices ham, heated
1 recipe Hollandaise sauce

Hollandaise Sauce:
3 egg yolks
2 tablespoons lemon juice
½ teaspoon salt
dash of pepper
1 stick butter, softened
½ cup boiling water

Place egg yolks, lemon juice, salt, pepper and butter in blender; blend for 15 seconds. While blender is running, carefully add boiling water. Pour the sauce into the top pan of a double boiler. Cook over boiling water, stirring constantly until sauce thickens.

Toast English muffins; lightly butter all 6 halves; place in a warmed, shallow serving dish. Place one slice of ham on each muffin half; cover with a poached egg. Pour sauce over all and serve hot.

P.C.Q. #16

To what President is the following attributed?
"You can fool some of the people some of the time, and some of the people all of the time, but you cannot fool all of the people all of the time."
a) Bill Clinton
b) Richard Nixon
c) Abraham Lincoln

McLarty's Mighty Mack: The Boss's Favorite

A stick-to-your-ribs power lunch!

Take the motorcade to the drive-thru at the local burger joint and get the Big Guy:

> *2 double cheeseburgers*
> *1 extra large order of fries*
> *1 large diet cola*

P.S. Don't let Hillary know when Bill has this — she gets mad and says it's bad press for a President who is so concerned with healthcare.

P.C.Q. #17

The Median Age of the Clinton White House Staff is:
a) 13
b) 21
c) 30 something
d) 42

GEORGE'S STEPHANOKOPITA

A real show-off number!

½ *pound Feta cheese*
4 ounces cream cheese
2 eggs
2 tablespoons parsley, chopped
1 teaspoon nutmeg
4 ounces Monterey Jack cheese
1 — 10 ounce package frozen, chopped spinach
1 medium onion, chopped
2 tablespoons butter
1 pound phyllo pastry
12 tablespoons melted butter

Thaw spinach and drain well. In food processor, blend Feta cheese, cream cheese, eggs, parsley, nutmeg and Monterey Jack cheese. Combine with spinach. Sauté onion in the 2 tablespoons butter; add to the spinach mixture. Cut the phyllo sheets to fit a 9" x 12" baking dish.

Butter dish and layer 10 sheets of phyllo, brushing each layer with melted butter. Spread with ¼ of the spinach mixture, top with 5 sheets of phyllo, brushing each with melted butter. Spread another ¼ of the spinach mixture over phyllo, layer another 5 sheets of phyllo, brushing each with melted butter. Continue, alternating spinach mixture and buttered phyllo, ending with 10 sheets of phyllo. Chill 1 hour.

Cut into 2" diamond shapes; place on baking sheet. Bake at 350° for 45 minutes until browned and crisp. Better grab one while you can, these won't last!

WEEKENDS AT BERNIE'S

*Sleep late then linger over
a delicious brunch...ahhh!*

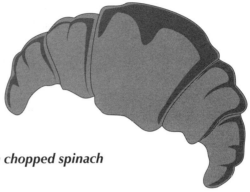

2 – 10-ounce packages frozen chopped spinach
4 tablespoons butter
4 tablespoons flour
2 cups milk
1 cup grated Cheddar cheese
8 eggs
Salt and pepper
Grated Parmesan cheese

Cook frozen spinach, drain well; place in a quiche dish in warm oven to keep hot. Melt butter in a sauce pan; add flour and stir for 2-3 minutes over low heat. Gradually add milk and stir; bring to a low boil, stirring constantly. Stir in Cheddar cheese and season with salt and pepper; keep warm. Poach eggs; arrange on top of spinach. Pour cheese sauce over eggs. Sprinkle with parmesan cheese and place under broiler until lightly browned. Serve immediately.

*Fresh melon and strawberries and buttery croissants
are the perfect additions to a delicious brunch table!*

WHITE-HOUSE-LEEKS SOUP!

Steamy and Satisfying!

2 leeks
3 potatoes, peeled and quartered
1 $\frac{2}{3}$ cups milk
$\frac{1}{3}$ cup cream
2 tablespoons butter
Salt and pepper

   Cut green part off of leeks, discard. Cut white part of leeks into small pieces; place in a heavy skillet; add enough water to cover. Bring to a boil; boil until tender; reserve water. In a saucepan boil potatoes until tender; drain; cool. Put leeks, water and cooled potatoes into blender; mix until smooth. Pour back into skillet; add salt, pepper, milk, cream and butter. Heat and serve. Serves 6.

★ ★

DEE DEE MYERS' MEDIA BLINTZES

*No time to spare
when the blintz hits the pan.*

4 eggs	1 pound cottage cheese
1 cup flour	3 ounces cream cheese
1 cup milk	$\frac{1}{8}$ teaspoon salt
$\frac{1}{4}$ teaspoon salt	2 tablespoons sugar
1 stick butter	

Mix eggs, flour, milk and salt to make a smooth batter. Let stand for 15 minutes. In a mixing bowl, beat together the cottage cheese, cream cheese, salt and sugar to make filling; set aside.

Heat a 7-inch skillet, grease with the stick of butter, to form a thin coat of melted butter; set butter stick aside. Pour enough of the batter into the frying pan to thinly coat the bottom. Cook on medium heat until lightly browned on bottom. Turn out onto waxed paper, browned side up. Place 2 tablespoons filling near one edge; turn in sides and roll. Repeat until all batter is used, greasing pan with stick of butter before pouring batter each time. Refrigerate rolled blintzes.

Just before serving, fry blintzes in buttered pan, turning until browned evenly on all sides.

Serve with sour cream and cinnamon.

HILLARY'S HEALTH-NUT COOKIES

Making these is almost as much fun as making sweeping changes in national domestic policy.

"I could have stayed home and baked cookies and had teas..."

1 cup flour
½ teaspoon baking soda
½ teaspoon salt
¼ teaspoon baking powder
½ teaspoon cinnamon
½ cup butter, softened

1 cup brown sugar
½ cup granulated sugar
1 egg, beaten
1 teaspoon vanilla extract
1 cup whole-grain
   cereal flakes
1 cup quick-cooking oats

In a small bowl, sift together the first five ingredients. In a mixing bowl, cream together butter and sugars. Add the egg and vanilla. Mix in cereal flakes and oats; stir in flour mixture.

Drop by rounded teaspoonfuls onto **far-left side** of greased cookie sheet, placing cookies about 4" apart. **Move a couple of cookies toward the center. Do not get close to the far-right!**

Using a spatula that has been dipped in water, flatten dough balls until they are paper thin. Bake at 350° for 8 to 10 minutes. Remove from cookie sheet while still warm; roll each cookie into a tube shape. Cookies become crisp as they cool.

With a cup of tea, these are a delicious pick-me-up during those long Congressional hearings!

★★★★★★★★★★★★★★★★★★★★★★★★★★★★★★★

IRA MAGAZINER'S
HEALTH CARE SHAKE-UP

A tough one to swallow.

1 tablespoon honey   *⅓ banana*
1 tablespoon wheat germ oil   *orange juice*
½ teaspoon brewer's yeast   *crushed ice*

Combine first 4 ingredients in a blender. Add orange juice to make 1 cup. Add 1 cup crushed ice. Blend well.

If we can make this drink available to every man, woman, and child in this country, America will be a healthier nation!

★★★★★★★★★★★★★★★★★★★★★★★★★★★★★★★★★

SURGEON GENERAL'S WIENER WRAPS AND CONDOMENTS

Let the kids help — you're never too young to wrap a wiener.

1 – 8 count package crescent roll dough
4 squares American cheese
8 wieners
Mustard
Assorted condoments

You want me to wear what?!!

Open crescent roll package, remove dough in one piece. Unroll and separate triangles of dough; spread each with 1 teaspoon of mustard. Cut each slice of cheese diagonally to make 8 triangles; place one piece on each of the 8 triangles of crescent dough. Place 1 wiener at the long edge of each triangle. Roll the dough and wiener up together, tucking the pointed end under. DON'T WORRY ABOUT A FEW HOLES IN THE DOUGH, YOUR WEINER WILL BE FINE. Place the wrapped wieners on a baking sheet; bake at 375° for 10 minutes.

Serve hot from the oven with chips and cold sodas. Be generous in distributing the condoments. The youngsters will thank you!

Warren Christopher's Protocoliflower Soup

A bit bland; but smooth, consistent and predictable.

1 large head cauliflower
2 tablespoons butter
1 medium onion, chopped
2 cans chicken broth
3 cups milk
1 tablespoon dried parsley
1 tablespoon dried chives
$\frac{1}{2}$ teaspoon dried thyme
$\frac{1}{2}$ pound grated Swiss cheese
Salt and pepper to taste

Cook cauliflower in boiling, salted water until tender. Drain, cool and coarsely chop cauliflower. Sauté onion in butter in a large saucepan. When onion is tender, add chopped cauliflower, chicken broth, milk, and herbs. Heat thoroughly; do not boil. Just before serving, add Swiss cheese, stir gently until melted. Add salt and pepper to taste.

Crusty French bread and a bottle of Chardonnay are appropriate complements.

P.C.Q. #18

Before his appointment as Secretary of State Warren Christopher was:
a) dull
b) very dull
c) very, very dull

BUREAU OF ALCOHOL TOBACCO AND FIREARMS TIPS FOR GRILLING

When preparing foods on the grill, safety is the most important consideration. Be sure that you follow the manufacturer's directions for safe operation of a gas or charcoal grill. Be sure that your grill is located outside in an area away from the house and other structures. Be sure that the grill is in an area away from where children may encounter it. Teach children to stay away from the grill, even if it does not appear to be hot. Charcoal stays hot even overnight!

1. *Be sure that the grill is in a safe location.*
2. *Check to be sure that the legs and racks are balanced and secure.*
3. *Spread charcoal briquettes in a single layer to extend slightly beyond the area needed for the amount of food to be grilled.*
4. *Mound the briquettes in the center of the rack.*
5. *Squirt approved charcoal starter over the coals. NEVER use gasoline or kerosene, as these are very explosive!*
6. *Allow starter fluid to soak into charcoal for a couple of minutes before lighting. NEVER add starter fluid after you have lit the coals.*
7. *Leave the briquettes in a mound until they turn whitish-gray in color, about 30 minutes.*
8. *Using fire-safe, long-handled tongs, spread the coals in an even layer on rack. A long-handled set of grilling tools is essential equipment for successful grilling.*
9. *Carefully place grilling rack into grill. Add foods to be grilled.*
10. *Watch foods carefully and follow instructions to ensure that meats are thoroughly and safely cooked.*

Janet Reno's Texas Barbeque

Hot Stuff!

1¼ cups tomato paste
⅓ cup vinegar
⅓ cup brown sugar
4 cloves garlic, minced
2 tablespoons chili powder
2 tablespoons prepared mustard
6 pounds beef ribs, cut into 3-rib sections

In a saucepan combine all ingredients except ribs; bring to a boil, turn down heat and simmer for 5 minutes. Wrap ribs in heavy foil, and grill over hot fire for 1 hour. Pour out any fat. Remove foil and return ribs to grill. Baste with barbeque sauce and cook an additional 15 minutes, turning once. Serve with additional warm barbeque sauce and plenty of napkins.

P.C.Q. #19

Before her appointment as Attorney General Janet Reno was:
a) a volunteer firefighter
b) a star of the Florida Gator Rodeo
c) an accomplished Florida attorney

FBI's Most Wanted: Mace Cookies

An all-natural and delicious
alternative to handguns.

½ teaspoon salt	2 eggs
1 teaspoon mace	2 tablespoons sour milk
3 cups flour	1 teaspoon soda
1 cup sugar	½ cup walnuts, chopped
1 cup butter, softened	Granulated sugar

Sift salt, mace and flour together; cut in butter and sugar with a pastry blender until crumbly. Add eggs and mix well. Dissolve soda in milk; add to other mixture. Add nuts. Drop by teaspoonful onto greased cookie sheet; flatten with a fork dipped in sugar. Sprinkle with additional sugar. Bake at 350° for 15 minutes.

Carry a supply of these in your pocket or handbag to munch on while riding the subway.

DEA'S "JUST SAY NO" SCRAMBLED BRAINS AND EGGS

2 sets brains
¼ teaspoon salt
½ teaspoon paprika
2 cloves garlic, crushed
⅓ cup flour
8 eggs
½ cup milk
⅛ teaspoon black pepper

Soak brains for 2 hours in cold water. Brains will be very mushy. Place in pan, cover with water and simmer for 20 minutes, do not boil. Let the brains cool for 20 minutes in the water. Drain. Cut brains in two lengthwise, dry on paper tow———

*Oh yuck! This recipe just gets more and more gross! Who wants to fry brains, gag! And put gooey eggs in with the mushy brains, give me a break, will you! Please — **Just Say No** to this one!*

CISNEROS' RELLANOS

A south-of-the-border classic; captures the heat of the Southwest sun.

1 pound ground beef
½ cup chopped onion
1½ teaspoons salt
⅛ teaspoon pepper
2 – 4-ounce cans green chilies
1½ cups milk
4 eggs
¼ cup flour
6 ounces shredded Cheddar cheese

Brown the ground beef with chopped onion, drain. Sprinkle with 1 teaspoon of the salt and the pepper. Drain chilies, split in half lengthwise. Place half of the chilies in a 10" x 6" x 2" baking dish. Sprinkle with shredded cheese; top with meat mixture. Arrange remaining chilies over meat. Combine milk, flour, eggs and ½ teaspoon salt; stir in a dash of pepper. Pour egg mixture over chilies. Bake at 350° for 40 to 50 minutes or until a knife inserted comes out clean. Serves 6.

Sliced tomatoes, cornbread and fresh fruit make this a fabulous brunch or supper!

P.C.Q. #20

Before his appointment as Agriculture Secretary Mike Espy was:
a) an Iowa corn farmer
b) an Arkansas hog farmer
c) U.S. Congressman from Mississippi

P.C.Q. #21

Before his appointment as Commerce Secretary Ron Brown was:
a) very wealthy
b) President of an international bank
c) Chairman of the National Democratic Party

RON BROWN'S HIGH LIVERS' PATÉ

Live high off the hog!

½ pound liverwurst
1 can condensed beef consomme
2 tablespoons brandy
1 envelope plain gelatin
1 teaspoon soy sauce
½ cup pitted black olives
⅓ cup fresh parsley leaves

Place gelatin in bowl of food processor; pour in ½ cup consomme; stir. Heat remaining consomme to boiling; pour into processor; stir to dissolve gelatin. Add remaining ingredients; process until smooth. Pour into a decorative mold and chill at least 4 hours. To serve, unmold on decorative tray and garnish with fresh sprigs of parsley. Serve with wafers and rounds of melba toast.

ROBERT'S REISCH PUDDING

Short on labor, long on flavor!

3 cups milk
½ cup sugar
2 cups cooked rice
3 tablespoons butter
1 teaspoon vanilla extract
½ cup raisins

In medium saucepan, combine milk, sugar, rice and butter; simmer for 30 minutes until thick. Remove from heat, stir in vanilla and raisins.

*A sweet treat, and so affordable —
even for the minimum wage earner.*

P.C.Q. #22

*Before his appointment as
Labor Secretary
Robert Reisch was:*
a) Steward, Local 1560 UAW
b) a jockey at Saratoga Springs
c) a Harvard professor

WHO'S MINDING THE MINTS?

Lloyd Bentsen
Secretary of the Treasury

⅔ cup sweetened, condensed milk
1 stick butter
1 stick margarine
2 pounds powdered sugar
3 drops oil of peppermint
Green food coloring

Mix together all ingredients except food coloring; blend with hands until dough-like. Divide dough into small batches and use several drops of green food coloring to color as desired; mix well. Pinch off small amounts; roll in granulated sugar; press into molds. Lay out on paper towel to dry. Makes approximately 200 mints.

If you run short, it's so easy to just
crank out more and more and more.....

RICHARD RILEY'S PUBLIC SCHOOL LUNCH LOAF

Ham Loaf, Snowflake Potatoes, Peas, Brownie and Milk

40 pounds ground pork
40 pounds ground ham
80 eggs, beaten
10 quarts pineapple juice or milk
40 cups cracker crumbs
10 teaspoons ground pepper

Mix all ingredients well. Pack into 40 loaf pans. Bake at 350° for 2 hours, basting often with glaze.

For glaze, combine the following and cook over medium heat until bubbly.

5 quarts pineapple juice
20 cups crushed pineapple
40 cups brown sugar
40 teaspoons mustard
10 teaspoons cloves
80 tablespoons vinegar

This will serve a whole schoolful of hungry, public-school kids. To make this at home, divide all quantities by 40.

DONNA SHALALA'S PASTA PRIMA-DONNA

A take charge dish!

½ pound fettucine
1 cup broccoli florets
¾ cup asparagus tips
1 small can ripe olives, sliced
¾ cup fresh green beans, cut into 1" pieces
½ cup sliced mushrooms
1 cup cherry tomatoes, sliced

Sauce:
2 cloves garlic, minced
½ cup butter
¾ cup half and half
⅔ cup grated Parmesan cheese
Salt and pepper

Place fettucine in one basket of a large steamer; steam over boiling water for 7 minutes. Place vegetables, except cherry tomatoes, in another basket; add to steamer and steam for 4 minutes; add cherry tomatoes; steam 2 minutes.

While pasta and vegetables are steaming, sauté garlic in butter in a medium-hot wok. Turn heat down to low; add heavy cream and Parmesan cheese; stir to mix well.

At the end of specified steaming time, combine vegetables with the sauce in the wok. Toss gently with fettucine. Transfer to a buttered pasta platter. Season with salt and fresh pepper; sprinkle LIBERALLY with additional grated Parmesan cheese.

With a salad of marinated red onion and cucumbers,
pungent garlic bread, and a full-bodied Chianti,
this meal makes a strong statement!

LEON PANETTA'S HI-RISE CAKE WITH NO-TRICKLE-DOWN FROSTING

What goes up, stays up!

For Cake:
1 package yellow cake mix
1 package instant lemon pudding
¾ cup vegetable oil
4 eggs
¾ cup orange juice

For Frosting:
4 tablespoons butter
3 cups powdered sugar
2 tablespoons lemon juice
1-2 tablespoons water
Few grains of salt

Grease and flour two 9-inch pans. In mixer bowl combine cake mix, pudding mix, oil, eggs, and orange juice. Beat at medium speed for 2 minutes. Pour into pans. Bake at 350° for 35 to 40 minutes. Remove onto wire racks and cool thoroughly.

Cream butter; add sugar gradually; cream thoroughly. Beat in lemon juice and just enough water to make of spreading consistency. Frosting should be stiff. Beat in salt. Spread on cooled cake.

*Slice and enjoy with a scoop of vanilla ice cream
and a steaming cup of coffee — Yum!*

★ ★

F.E.M.A. FAVORITE:
TORNADOES DE BOEUF

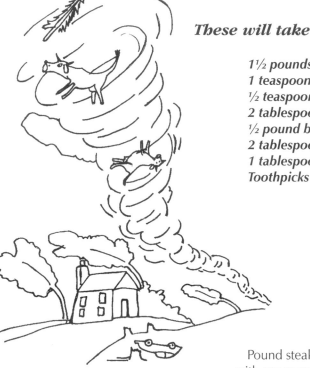

These will take your guests by storm!

1½ pounds flank steak
1 teaspoon garlic salt
½ teaspoon black pepper
2 tablespoons soy sauce
½ pound bacon, cooked slightly
2 tablespoons parsley flakes
1 tablespoon tarragon leaves
Toothpicks

Pound steak to ½" thickness. Sprinkle with soy sauce, garlic salt and pepper. Place bacon strips on meat and sprinkle with parsley and tarragon. Beginning at small end, roll meat tightly, securing with toothpicks along the roll. Cut roll into 1" wide pinwheels. Grill to desired doneness.

Serve with fluffy, hot rice and a crisp green salad.

P.C.Q. #23

FEMA stands for:
a) the name of the human thigh bone.
b) a national women's rights organization.
c) the Federal Emergency Management Administration.

★ ★

DEPARTMENT OF TRANSPORTATION'S ROCKY ROAD CAKE

***Surely the road to ruin
for the calorie counter!***

1 cup chopped walnuts
1 cup seedless raisins
1 cup miniature marshmallows
1 package Devil's food cake mix,
  with pudding in the mix
4 eggs
1 cup real mayonnaise
1 cup water
Powdered sugar

Grease and flour a 12 cup bundt pan. In a small bowl mix walnuts, raisins and marshmallows. In mixer bowl combine cake mix, eggs, mayonnaise and water. Beat at medium speed for 2 minutes. Pour into prepared pan. Bake at 350° for 50 minutes. Cool in pan for 15 minutes. Invert on rack, cool. Dust with powdered sugar.

*To serve, place a generous slice of cake on each dessert dish,
top with a scoop of chocolate ice cream, drizzle with
chocolate syrup and crown with a walnut half.
Decadent!*

Abercrombie, Neil (D) Hawaii • Ackerman, Gary L. (D) New York • Allard, Wayne (R) Colorado • Andrews, Michael A. (D) Texas • Andrews, Robert E. (D) New Jersey • Andrews, Thomas H. (D) Maine • Applegate, Douglas (D) Ohio • Archer, Bill (R) Texas • Armey, Richard K. (R) Texas • Aspin, Les (D) Wisconsin • Bacchus, Jim (D) Florida • Bachus, Spencer T.,III (R) Alabama • Baesler, Scotty (D) Kentucky • Baker, Bill (R) California • Baker, Richard H. (R) Louisiana • Ballenger, Cass (R) North Carolina • Barcia, James A. (D) Michigan • Barlow, Thomas J. III (D) Kentucky • Barrett, Bill (R) Nebraska • Barrett, Thomas M. (D) Wisconsin • Bartlett, Roscoe G. (R) Maryland • Barton, Joe (R) Texas • Bateman, Herbert H. (R) Virginia • Becerra, Xavier (D) California • Beilenson, Anthony C. (D) California • Bentley, Helen Delich (R) Maryland • Bereuter, Doug (R) Nebraska • Berman, Howard L. (D) California • Bevill, Tom (D) Alabama • Bilbray, James H. (D) Nevada • Bilirakis, Michael (R) Florida • Bishop, Sanford D.,Jr. (D) Georgia • Blackwell, Lucien E. (D) Pennsylvania • Bliley, Thomas J., Jr. (R) Virginia • Blute, Peter (R) Massachusetts • Boehlert, Serwood L. (R) New York • Boehner, John A. (R) Ohio • Bonilla, Henry (R) Texas • Bonior, David E. (D) Michigan • Borski, Robert A. (D) Pennsylvania • Boucher, Rick (D) Virginia • Brewster, Bill K. (D) Oklahoma • Brooks, Jack (D) Texas • Browder, Glen (D) Alabama • Brown, Corrinne (D) Florida • Brown, George E., Jr (D) California • Brown, Sherrod (D) Ohio • Bryant, John (D) Texas • Bunning, Jim (R) Kentucky • Burton, Dan (R) Indiana • Buyer, Steven E. (R) Indiana • Byrne, Leslie L. (D) Virginia • Callahan, Sonny (R) Alabama • Calvert, Ken (R) California • Camp, Dave (R) Michigan • Canady, Charles T. (R) Florida • Cantwell, Maria (D) Washington • Cardin, Benjamin L. (D) Maryland • Carr, Bob (D) Michigan • Castle, Michael N. (R) Delaware • Chapman, Jim (D) Texas • Clay, William (D) Missouri • Clayton, Eva M. (D) North Carolina • Clement, Bob (D) Tennessee • Clinger, William F.,Jr.(R) Pennsylvania • Clyburn, James E. (D) South Carolina • Coble, Howard (R) North Carolina • Coleman, Ronald D. (D) Texas • Collins, Barbara-Rose (D) Michigan • Collins, Cardiss (D) Illinois • Collins, Michael A. (R) Georgia • Combest, Larry (R) Texas • Condit, Gary A. (D) California • Conyers, John, Jr. (D) Michigan • Cooper, Jim (D) Tennessee • Coppersmith, Sam (D) Arizona • Costello, Jerry F. (D) Illinois • Cox, Christopher (R) California • Coyne, William J. (D) Pennsylvania • Cramer, Robert E. (Bud)(D) Alabama • Crane, Philip M. (R) Illinois • Crapo, Michael D. (R) Idaho • Cunningham, Randy (R) California • Danner, Pat (D) Missouri • Darden, George (D) Georgia • Deal, Nathan (D) Georgia • DeFazio, Peter A. (D) Oregon • de la Garza, E. (D) Texas • DeLauro, Rosa L. (D) Connecticut • DeLay, Tom (R) Texas • Dellums, Ronald V. (D) California • de Lugo, Ron (D) Virgin Islands • Derrick, Butler (D) South Carolina • Deutsch, Peter (D) Florida • Diaz-Balart, Lincoln (R) Florida • Dickey, Jay (R) Arizona • Dicks, Norman D. (D) Washington • Dingell, John D. (D) Michigan • Dixon, Julian C. (D) California • Dooley, Calvin M. (D) California • Doolittle, John T. (R) California • Dornan, Robert K. (R) California • Dreir, David (R) California • Duncan, John J, Jr. (R) California • Dunn, Jennifer (R) Washington • Durbin, Richard J. (D) Illinois • Edwards, Chet (D) Texas • Edwards, Don (D) California • Emerson, Bill (R) Missouri • Engel, Eliot (D) New York • English, Glenn (D) Oklahoma • English, Karan (D) Arizona • Eshoo, Anna G. (D) California • Espy, Mike (D) Mississippi • Evans, Lane (D) Illinois • Everett, Terry (R) Alaska • Ewing, Thomas W. (R) Illinois • Faleomavaega, Eni F.H. (D) American Somalia • Fawell, Harris W. (R) Illinois • Fazio, Vic (D) California • Fields, Cleo (D) Louisiana • Fields, Jack (R) Texas • Filner, Bob (D) California • Fingerhut, Eric (D) Ohio • Fish, Hamilton, Jr. (R) New York • Flake, Floyd H. (D) New York • Foglietta, Thomas M. (D) Pennsylvania • Foley, Thomas S. (D) Washington • Ford, Harold E. (D) Tennessee • Ford, William D. (D) Michigan • Fowler, Tillie K. (R) Florida • Frank, Barney (D) Maryland • Franks, Bob (R) New Jersey • Franks, Gary A. (R) Connecticut • Frost, Martin (D) Texas • Furse, Elizabeth (D) Oregon • Gallegly, Elton (R) California • Gallo, Dean A. (R) New Jersey • Gejdenson, Sam (D) Connecticut • Gekas, George W. (R) Pennsylvania • Gephardt, Richard A. (D) Missouri • Geren, Pete (D) Texas • Gibbons, Sam (D) Florida • Gilchrest, Wayne T. (R) Maryland • Gillmor, Paul E. (R) Ohio • Gilman, Benjamin A. (R) New York • Gingrich, Newt (R) Georgia • Glickman, Dan (D) Kansas • Gonzalez, Henry B. (D) Texas • Goodlatte, Bob (R) Virginia • Goodling, William F. (R) Pennsylvania • Gordon, Bart (D) Tennessee • Goss, Porter J. (R) Florida • Grams, Rod (R) MN • Grandy, Fred (R) IA • Green, Gene (D) Texas • Greenwood, James C. (R) Pennsylvania • Gunderson, Steve (R) Wisconsin • Gutierrez, Luis V. (D) Illinois • Hall, Ralph M. (D) Texas • Hall, Tony P. (D) Ohio • Hamburg, Dan (D) California • Hamilton, Lee H. (D) Indiana • Hancock, Mel (R) Missouri • Hansen, James V. (R) Utah • Harman, Jane (D) California • Hastert, J. Dennis (R) Illinois • Hastings, Alcee L. (D) Florida • Hayes, James A. (D) Louisiana • Hefley, Joel (R) Colorado • Hefner, W.G. (D) North Carolina • Henry, Paul B. (R) Michigan • Herger, Wally (R) California • Hilliard, Earl F. (D) Alabama • Hinchey, Maurice D. (D) New York • Hoagland, Peter (D) Nebraska • Hobson, David L. (R) Ohio • Hochbrueckner, George (D) New York • Hoekstra, Peter (R) Michigan • Hoke, Martin R. (R) Ohio • Holden, Tim (D) Pennsylvania • Horn, Stephen (R) California • Houghton, Amo (R) New York • Hoyer, Steny H. (D) MD • Huffington, Michael (R) California • Hughes, Willaim J. (D) New Jersey • Hunter, Duncan (R) California • Hutchinson, Y. Tim (R) Arizona • Hutto, Earl (D) Florida • Hyde, Henry (R) Illinois • Inglis, Bob (R) South Carolina • Inhofe, James M. (R) Oklahoma • Inslee, Jay (D) Washington • Istook, Ernest J., Jr. (R) Oklahoma • Jacobs, Andrew, Jr. (D) Indiana • Jefferson, William J. (D) Louisiana • Johnson, Don (D) Georgia • Johnson, Eddie Bernice (D) Texas • Johnson, Nancy L. (R) Connecticut • Johnson, Sam (R) Texas • Johnson, Tim (D) South Dakota • Johnston, Harry (D) Florida • Kanjorski, Paul E. (D) Pennsylvania • Kaptur, Marcy (D) Ohio • Kasich, John R. (R) Ohio • Kennedy, Joseph P. III (D) Massachusetts • Kennelly, Barbara B. (D) Connecticut • Kildee, Dale E. (D) Michigan • Kim, Jay (R) California • King, Peter T. (R) New York • Kingston, Jack (R) Georgia • Kleczka, Gerald D. (D) Wisconsin • Klein, Herb (D) New Jersey • Klink, Ron (D) Pennsylvania • Klug, Scott L. (R) Wisconsin • Knollenberg, Joe (R) Michigan • Kolbe, Jim (R) Arizona • Kopetski, Michael J. (D) Oregon • Kreidler, Mike (D) Washington • Kyl, Jon (R) Arizona • LaFalce, John J. (D) New York • Lambert, Blanche M. (D) Arizona • Lancaster, H. Martin (D) North Carolina • Lantos, Tom (D) California • LaRocco, Larry (D) Idaho • Laughlin, Greg (D) Texas • Lazio, Rick (R) New York • Leach, James A. (R) Iowa • Lehman, Richard H. (D) California • Levin, Sander M. (D) Michigan • Levy, David A. (R) New York • Lewis, Jerry (R) California • Lewis, John (D) Georgia • Lewis, Tom (R) Florida • Lightfoot, Jim (R) Iowa • Linder, John (R) Georgia • Lipinski, William O. (D) Illinois • Livingston, Bob (R) Louisiana • Lloyd, Marilyn (D) Tennessee • Long, Jill L. (D) Indiana • Lowey, Nita M. (D) New York • McCandless, Alfred A. (R) California • McCloskey, Frank (D) Indiana • McCollum, Bill (R) Florida • McCrery, Jim (R) Louisiana • McCurdy, Dave (D) Oklahoma • McDade, Joseph M. (R) Pennsylvania • McDermott, Jim (D) Washington • McHale, Paul (D) Pennsylvania • McHugh, John M. (R) New York • McInnis, Scott (R) Colorado • McKeon, Howard P. (R) California • McKinney, Cynthia A. (D) Georgia • McMillan, J. Alex (R) North Carolina • McNulty, Michael R. (D) New York • Machtley, Ronald K. (R) Rhode Island • Maloney, Carolyn B. (D) New York • Mann, David (D) Ohio • Manton, Thomas J. (D) New York • Manzullo, Donald A. (R) Illinois • Margolies-Mezvinsky, M.(D) Pennsylvania • Markey, Edward J. (D) Massachusetts • Martinez, Matthew G. (D) California • Matsui, Robert T. (D) California • Mazzoli, Romano L. (D) Kentucky • Meehan, Martin T. (D) Massachusetts • Meek, Carrie P, (D) Florida • Menendez, Robert (D) New Jersey • Meyers, Jan (R) Kansas • Mfume, Kweisi (D) Maryland • Mica, John L. (R) Florida • Michel, Robert H. (R) Illinois • Miller, Dan (R) Florida • Miller, George (D) California • Mineta, Norman Y. (D) California • Minge, David (D) MN • Mink, Patsy T. (D) Hawaii • Moakley, John Joseph (D) MA • Molinari, Susan (R) New York • Mollohan, Alan B. (D) West Virginia • Montgomery, G.V. (D) MSMoorhead, Carlos J. (R) California • Moran, James P. (D) Virginia • Morella, Constance A. (R) Maryland • Murphy, Austin J. (D) Pennsylvania • Murtha, John P, (D) Pennsylvania • Myers, John T. (R) Indiana • Nadler, Jerrold (D) New York • Natcher, William H. (D) Kentucky • Neal, Richard E. (D) Massachusetts • Neal, Stephen L. (D) North Carolina • Norton, Eleanor Holmes (D) District of Columbia • Nussle, Jim (R) Iowa • Oberstar, James L. (D) MN • Obey, David R. (D) Wisconsin • Olver, John W. (D) Massachusetts • Oritz, Solomon P. (D) Texas • Orton, Bill (D) Utah • Owens, Major R. (D) New York • Oxley, Michael G. (R) Ohio • Packard, Ron (R) California • Pallone, Frank Jr. (D) New Jersey • Panetta, Leon E. (D) California • Parker, Mike (D) MSPastor Ed (D) Arizona • Paxon, Bill (R) New York • Payne, Donald M. (D) New Jersey • Payne, L.F. (D) Virginia • Pelosi, Nancy (D) California • Penny, Timothy J. (D) MN • Peterson, Collin C. (D) MN • Peterson, Douglas (D) Florida • Petri, Thomas E. (R) Wisconsin • Pickett, Owen B. (D) Virginia • Pickle, J.J. (D) Texas • Pombo, Richard W. (R) California • Pomeroy, Earl (D) North Dakota • Porter, John Edward (R) Illinois • Poshard Glenn (D) Illinois • Price, David E. (D) North Carolina • Pryce, Deborah (R) Ohio • Quillen, James H. (R) Tennessee • Quinn, Jack (R) New York • Rahall, Nick J., II (D) West Virginia • Ramstad, Jim (R) MN • Rangel, Charles B. (D) New York • Ravenel, Arthur, Jr. (R) South Carolina • Reed, Jack (D) Rhode Island • Regula, Ralph (R) Ohio • Reynolds, Mel (D) Illinois • Richardson, Bill (D) New Mexico • Ridge, ThomasJ. (R) Pennsylvania • Roberts, Pat (R) Kansas • Roemer, Tim (D) Indiana • Rogers, Harold (R) Kentucky • Rohrabacher, Dana (R) California • Romero-Barcelo, Carlos (D) Puerto Rico • Ros-Legtinen, Ileana (R) Florida • Rose, Charlie (D) North Carolina • Rostenkowski, Dan (D) Illinois • Roth, Toby (R) Wisconsin • Roukema, Marge (R) New Jersey • Rowland, J. Roy (D) Georgia • Roybal-Allard, Lucille (D) California • Royce, Edward R. (R) California • Rush, Bobby L. (D) Illinois • Sabo, Martin Olav (D) MN • Sanders, Bernard (I) Vermont • Sangmeister, George E. (D) Illinois • Santorum, Rick (R) Pennsylvania • Sarpalius, Bill (D) Texas • Sawyer, Thomas C. (D) Ohio • Saxton, Jim (R) New Jersey • Schaefer, Dan (R) Colorado • Schenk, Lynn (D) California • Schiff, Steven (R) New Mexico • Schroeder, Patricia (D) Colorado • Schumer, Charles E. (D) New York • Scott, Robert C. (D) Virginia • Sensenbrenner, F.J. Jr.(R) Wisconsin • Serrano, Jose E. (D) New York • Sharp, Phillip R. (D) Indiana • Shaw, E. Clay, Jr. (R) Florida • Shays, Christopher (R) Connecticut • Shepherd, Karen (D) Utah • Shuster, Bud (R) Pennsylvania • Sisisky, Norman (D) Virginia • Skaggs, David E. (D) Colorado • Skeen, Joe (R) New Mexico • Skelton, Ike (D) Missouri • Slattery, Jim (D) Kansas • Slaughter, L. McIntosh (D) New York • Smith, Christopher H. (R) New Jersey • Smith, Lamar S. (R) Texas • Smith, Neal (D) Iowa • Smith, Nick (R) Michigan • Smith, Robert F. (R) Oregon • Snowe, Olympia J. (R) Maine ME • Solomon, Gerald B.H. (R) New York • Spence, Floyd (R) South Carolina • Spratt, John M. Jr. (D) South Carolina • Stark, Fortney Pete (D) California • Stearns, Cliff (R) Florida • Stenholm, Charles W. (D) Texas • Stokes, Louis (D) Ohio • Strickland, Ted (D) Ohio • Studds, Gerry E. (D) Massachusetts • Stump, Bob (R) Arizona • Stupak, Bart (D) Michigan • Sundquist, Don (R) Tennessee • Swett, Dick (D) New Hampshire • Swift, Al (D) Washington • Synar, Mike (D) Oklahoma • Talent, James M. (R) Missouri • Tanner, John S. (D) Tennessee • Tauzin, W.J. (D) Lousiana • Taylor, Charles H. (R) North Carolina • Taylor, Gene (D) MS • Tejeda, Frank (D) Texas • Thomas, Craig (R) Wyoming • Thomas, William M. (R) California • Thornton, Ray (D) Arizona • Thurman, Karen L. (D) Florida • Torkildsen, Peter G. (R) Massachusetts • Torres, Esteban Edward (D) California • Torricelli, Robert G. (D) New Jersey • Towns, Edolphus (D) New York • Traficant, James A. Jr.(D) Ohio • Tucker, Walter R., III (D) California • Underwood, Robert A. (D) GU • Unsoeld, Jolene (D) Washington • Upton, Fred (R) Michigan • Valentine, Tim (D) North Carolina • Velazquez, Nydia M. (D) New York • Vento, Bruce F. (D) MN • Visclosky, Peter J. (D) Indiana • Volkmer, Harold L. (D) Missouri • Vucanovich, Barbara F. (R) Nevada • Walker, Robert S. (R) Pennsylvania • Walsh, James T. (R) New York • Washington, Craig A. (D) Texas • Waters, Maxine (D) California • Watt, Melvin (D) North Carolina • Waxman, Henry A. (D) California • Weldon, Curt (R) Pennsylvania • Wheat, Alan (D) Missouri • Whitten, Jamie L. (D) MS • Williams, Pat (D) Montana • Wilson, Charles (D) Texas • Wise, Robert E.,Jr. (D) West Virginia • Wolf, Frank R. (R) Virginia • Woolsey, Lynn C. (D) California • Wyden, Ron (D) Oregon • Wynn, Albert Russell (D) Maryland • Yates, Sidney R. (D) Illinois • Young, C.W. Bill (R) Florida • Young, Don (R) Alaska • Zeliff, William H., Jr.(R) New Hampshire • Zimmer, Dick (R) New Jersey •

Akaka, Daniel K. (D) Hawaii • Baucus, Max (D) Montana • Bennett,, Robert F. (R) Utah • Biden Joseph R., Jr. (D) Delaware • Bingaman, Jeff (D) New Mexico • Bond, Christoper S. Kit (R) Missouri • Boren, David L. (D) Oklahoma • Boxer, Barbara (D) California • Bradley, Bill (D) New Jersey • Breaux, John B. (D) Louisiana • Brown, Hank (R) Colorado • Bryan, Richard H. (D) Nevada • Bumpers, Dale (D) Arkansas • Burns, Conrad (R) Montana • Byrd, Robert C. (D) West Virginia • Campbell, Ben Nighthorse(D) Colorado • Chafee, John H. (R) Rhode Island • Coats, Daniel R. (R) Indiana • Cochran, Thad (R) Mississippi • Cohen, William S. (R) Maine • Conrad, Kent (D) North Dakota • Coverdell, Paul (R) Georgia • Craig, Larry (R) Idaho • D'Amato, Alfonse M. (R) New York • Danforth, John C. (R) Missouri • Daschle, Thomas A. (D) South Dakota • DeConcini, Dennis (D) Arizona • Dodd, Christopher J. (D) Connecticut • Dole, Robert (R) Kansas • Domenici, Pete V. (R) New Mexico • Dorgan, Byron L. (D) North Dakota • Durenberger, Dave (R) Minnesota • Exon, J. James (D) Nebraska • Faircloth, Lauch (R) North Carolina • Feingold, Russell (D) Wisconsin • Feinstein, Dianne (D) California • Ford, Wendell H. (D) Kentucky • Glenn, John (D) Ohio • Gorton, Slade (R) Washington • Graham, Robert (D) Florida • Gramm, Phil (R) Texas • Grassley, Charles E. (R) Iowa • Gregg, Judd (R) New Hampshire • Harkin, Tom (D) Iowa • Hatch, Orrin G. (R) Utah • Hatfield, Mark O. (R) Oregon • Heflin, Howell T. (D) Alabama • Helms, Jesse A. (R) North Carolina • Hollings, Ernest F. (D) South Carolina • Inouye, Daniel K. (D) Hawaii • Jeffords, James M. (R) Vermont • Johnston, J. Bennett,Jr.(D) Louisiana • Kassebaum, Nancy Landon (R) Kansas • Kempthorne, Dirk A. (R) Idaho • Kennedy, Edward M. (D) Massachusetts • Kerrey, Robert (D) Nebraska • Kerry, John F. (D) Massachusetts • Kohl, Herbert H. (D) Wisconsin • Krueger, Bob (D) Texas • Lautenberg, Frank R. (D) New Jersey • Leahy, Patrick J. (D) Vermont • Levin, Carl (D) Michigan • Lieberman, Joseph I. (D) Connecticut • Lott, Trent (R) Mississippi • Lugar, Richard G. (R) Indiana • Mack, Connie (R) Florida • Mathews, Harlan (D) Tennessee • McCain, John (R) Arizona • McConnell, Mitch (R) Kentucky • Metzenbaum, Howard M. (D) Ohio • Mikulski, Barbara A. (D) Maryland • Mitchell, George J. (D) Maine • Moseley-Braun, Carol (D) Illinois • Moynihan, Daniel Patrick(D) New York • Murkowski, Frank H. (R) Alaska • Murray, Patty (D) Washington • Nickles, Don (R) Oklahoma • Nunn, Sam (D) Georgia • Packwood, Bob (R) Oregon • Pell, Claiborne (D) Rhode Island • Pressler, Larry (R) South Dakota • Pryor, David (D) Arkansas • Reid, Harry M. (D) Nevada • Riegle, Donald W. Jr. (D) Michigan • Robb, Charles S. (D) Virginia • Rockefeller, John D. IV (D) West Virginia • Roth, William V. Jr. (R) Delaware • Sarbanes, Paul S. (D) Maryland • Sasser, Jim (D) Tennessee • Shelby, Richard C. (D) Alabama • Simon, Paul (D) Illinois • Simpson, Alan K. (R) Wyoming • Smith, Robert (R) New Hampshire • Specter, Arlen (R) Pennsylvania • Stevens, Ted (R) Alaska • Thurmond, Strom (R) South Carolina • Wallop, Malcolm (R) Wyoming • Warner, John W. (R) Virginia • Wellstone, Paul (D) Minnesota • Wofford, Harris (D) Pennsylvania.

CHAPTER FOUR
CAPITOL HILL CUISINE

SENATOR TED KENNEDY'S PARTY PUNCH
SENATOR PAUL SIMON'S BOW TIE STARTERS
SENATOR DIANNE FEINSTEIN'S FEMMINACHOS
SENATOR PATSY SCHROEDER'S S.O.S. DIP
SENATOR DENNIS DECONCINI'S SOUTHWEST SUNSET SPECIALTIES
THE FULL HOUSE SALAD
FEDERAL BUDGET STEAK WITH GRAVY
ISOLATIONIST CHICKEN
CONGRESSIONAL GRIDLOX AND BAGELS
SENATE CELERY INCREASE
DEMOCRATIC PRO-CHOYS PLATFORM
TERM-LIMIT TROUT
BUN CONTROL LEGISLATION
SENATOR ROBERT BYRD'S JURASSIC PORK
REPRESENTATIVE RICHARD GEPHARDT'S TAX AND SPEND SOUFFLE
SENATOR JIM SASSER'S DEFICIT STEW
NATIONAL GAS TAX BLUES
REPRESENTATIVE DAN ROSTENKOWSKI'S GAME'S-UP DINNER
SENATOR PATRICK LEAHY'S ST. PATTY'S DAY FEAST
SENATOR DANIEL PATRICK MOYNIHAN'S LEFTOVER-BLARNEY SUPPER
SENATOR CAROL MOSELEY-BRAUN'S WELFARE REFORM
SENATOR ERNEST HOLLINGS' TRUE-GRITS
REPRESENTATIVE MAXINE WATERS' PEACE AND HOMINY
'EARS TO YOU TOM FOLEY!
SENATOR BEN NIGHTHORSE CAMPBELL'S FRUITS OF THE LAND
SENATOR JOHN GLENN'S OUT-OF-THIS-WORLD BUCKEYES
SENATOR WENDELL FORD'S PRUNE WHIP
SENATOR HOWELL HEFLIN'S PRIDE OF THE SOUTH
CAPITOL FILLIBUSTER BARS
BI-PARTISAN-CHIP COOKIES
GERRRYMANDARIN DELIGHT
CONGRESSIONAL PERKS
HOUSE BANK HI-BOUNCERS

★★★★★★★★★★★★★★★★★★★★★★★★★★★★★★★★★★★★★★★

SENATOR TED KENNEDY'S PARTY PUNCH

This one packs a wallop.

Warning: Do not operate an automobile after consuming this beverage. Do not operate a watercraft after consuming this beverage. Do not attempt to operate an automobile *as* a watercraft after consuming this beverage.

1 – 48 ounce bottle cranberry juice
1 large can pineapple juice
1 cup orange juice
1 cup lemon juice
2 quarts ginger ale
Gin
1 thinly sliced orange, unpeeled

Chill all ingredients well. To serve, combine juices and ginger ale in a very large punch bowl. Add gin to taste; stir well. Gently float an ice ring in bowl; garnish with orange slices.

SENATOR PAUL SIMON'S BOW-TIE STARTERS

Be a trendsetter!

1 loaf thinly sliced sandwich bread
1 can condensed cream of asparagus soup
12 uncooked bacon strips, cut in half

Trim all crusts from bread. Spread condensed soup on one side of each bread slice. Roll up each slice of bread, beginning and ending at a corner. Wrap a half strip of bacon around the middle of each roll and secure with a toothpick. Place bow-ties on a baking sheet and bake at 250° for 1 hour. Makes 2 dozen.

SENATOR DIANNE FEINSTEIN'S FEMMINACHOS

Take note! These are powerful and they really stick together!

1 pound ground chuck
1 envelope taco seasoning
⅓ cup water
1½ cups shredded sharp Cheddar cheese
1 small can sliced pickled jalepeño peppers
1 medium tomato, chopped
⅓ cup sliced, pitted ripe olives
1 large bag white corn tortilla chips
½ cup sour cream
½ cup guacamole dip

In a hot skillet, brown the ground chuck; drain off fat. Add taco seasoning and water, stir. Cook until liquid is absorbed.

Pile a large mound of tortilla chips on a cookie sheet, making sure that chips are spread out, but still touching each other. Spread the seasoned beef over the chips. Sprinkle the cheese atop the beef. Place in 400° oven for 3 to 5 minutes, just until cheese melts, watch carefully! Remove from oven and carefully slide mound of nachos onto large serving plate.

Garnish with tomato, olives and jalepeños. Mound sour cream and guacamole into small bowls and serve alongside nachos. *OLÉ!*

P.C.Q. #24

Political analysts and the media dubbed 1992 the year of:
a) The chameleon
b) The Baboon
c) The Donkey
d) The Woman

★★★★★★★★★★★★★★★★★★★★★★★★★★★★★★★★★★★★★

SENATOR PATSY SCHROEDER'S S.Q.S. DIP

Putting women in combat would sure improve things in the Mess Tent!

8 ounces cream cheese, softened
2 tablespoons milk
¾ cup dried beef, chopped
1 tablespoon onion, minced
2 tablespoons green pepper, chopped
¼ teaspoon seasoned pepper
½ cup sour cream

In a medium bowl, blend together cream cheese and milk. Mix in dried beef, onion, green pepper, seasoned pepper and sour cream. Spoon into a small casserole. Bake at 350° for 15 minutes. To serve, keep warm on a hot plate or over a candle-type food warmer. Serve with a variety of crackers or melba toast rounds.

A delicious adaptation of an old Army standard — Innovative!

P.C.Q. #25

A Broad-Based Contribution is:
a) a charitable donation to a women's rights groups
b) a gift from the gals in the office
c) a tax increase

SENATOR DENNIS DECONCINI'S SOUTHWEST SUNSET SPECIALTIES

Time to retire and enjoy the good life.

— Fresh Salsa —

4 fresh dark green chili peppers
4 ripe tomatoes
1 small onion
1 — 16-ounce can tomato sauce
Salt to taste

Finely chop tomatoes, peppers and onions. Mix together in a bowl; stir in tomato sauce and salt. Cover and refrigerate for several hours. Let stand at room temperature for 1 hour before serving.

— Tortilla Chips —

10 flour or corn tortillas, cut into quarters
3 cups cooking oil
Salt

Heat oil in deep kettle. Fry tortilla quarters in oil, a few at a time, until crisp; drain on paper towel. Sprinkle with salt.

— Margarita —

3 ounces triple sec   *9 ounces Tequila*
6 ounces lime juice   *Salt*
6 ounces lemon juice   *½ lime, cut into wedges*

Mix all ingredients in blender. Place blender jar in freezer. To serve, rim glasses with salt and fill with crushed ice. Pour chilled Margarita over ice and garnish with a lime wedge.

THE FULL HOUSE SALAD

*A **delicious combination of crisp greens
and pungent accompaniments.**
A **satisfying meal in itself!***

1 small head Romaine lettuce
1 small head Boston lettuce
1 cup Prosciutto ham, cut in julienne strips
4 hearts of palm, chopped
1 sweet red pepper, diced
1 clove garlic, sliced
2 tablespoons Parmesan cheese

— Vinaigrette Dressing —
6 tablespoons olive oil
2 tablespoons wine vinegar
Juice of one lemon
2 teaspoons soy sauce
Pinch dry mustard
Salt and pepper to taste

P.C.Q. #26

NAFTA stands for:
a) a national chain of car parts
   stores.
b) "Now And Forever Aftah,"
   part of Sen. Ted Kennedy's
   wedding vows.
c) Vice President Al Gore's plan
   for reinventing government.
d) North American Free Trade
   Agreement between Canada,
   Mexico and the U.S.

Wash and trim lettuce; separate leaves and drain well. Lay on paper towels. Rub wooden salad bowl with garlic. Tear lettuce into bite-sized pieces; place in bowl; add Prosciutto, hearts of palm, red pepper and Parmesan cheese.

Combine all ingredients for dressing in a jar with a tight-fitting lid; shake well to mix. Gently toss salad with dressing.

FEDERAL BUDGET STEAK WITH GRAVY

A cost-cutting meal that keeps the flavor intact!

1 pound ground beef
¼ cup fine bread crumbs
1 egg, beaten
1 teaspoon salt
⅛ teaspoon pepper
3 tablespoons minced onions
¼ cup diced celery
2 tablespoons butter
1 can cream of mushroom soup,
    diluted with ½ can water

Combine ground beef with crumbs, egg, salt, pepper, onion and celery. Shape into oblong loaf, about 1 inch thick. Brown in butter in skillet. Carefully turn and brown on other side. Cover with diluted soup and cook on top of stove at medium-low temperature for 25-30 minutes.

P.C.Q. #27

President Clinton's National Service Plan...

a) Guarantees affordable automobile maintenance for every truck, bus and car made in America

b) Mandates military service for cross-dressing trisexuals.

c) Provides discreet, inexpensive, illegal aliens to serve as Nannies to the children of wealthy attorneys.

d) Provides tuition money to college students in exchange for service in national work programs.

ISOLATIONIST CHICKEN

Keep it controlled, Keep it protected,
Keep it covered.

4 chicken breasts, boneless and skinless
1 box long grain wild rice with herbs
1 can cream of mushroom soup
1 can mushrooms, drained
1 can cream of celery soup
1 can cold water
1 dash curry powder
1 packet onion soup mix

Mix rice, soups, water, parsley, curry powder and mushrooms in a lightly greased casserole. Place chicken on top; sprinkle onion soup mix on top. Seal with foil. Bake at 350° for 2 hours. Do not open foil during cooking time.

CONGRESSIONAL GRIDLOX AND BAGELS

This is one lunch that
everyone can agree on!

6 bagels, variety of flavors
1 — 8-ounce package cream cheese
1½ pounds lox
3 Kosher dill pickles, halved
Lettuce leaves
½ red onion, thinly sliced

Split bagels; generously spread both halves with cream cheese. Lay filets of lox on top of cream cheese on one bagel half. Garnish plate with lettuce leaf, half of a pickle, and onion slices.

SENATE CELERY INCREASE

*A real vote getter
in closed-door sessions!*

4 cups celery, cut in 1" pieces
½ cup blanched almonds, chopped
3 tablespoons butter
3 tablespoons flour
1½ cups chicken broth
½ cup cream
Salt
Pepper
Parmesan cheese
Bread crumbs

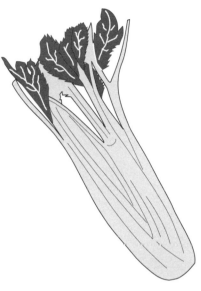

Parboil celery, drain. Place in buttered casserole with the chopped almonds. In a saucepan, melt butter; stir in flour; add chicken broth, cream, salt and pepper. Cook the sauce until thick; pour over celery. Sprinkle liberally with cheese; cover with bread crumbs. Bake at 350° for 25 minutes or until bubbly.

P.C.Q. #29

A joint session refers to:
a) Bill Clinton and his college pals rolling one and smoking, but not inhaling it, while discussing the evils of war in Vietnam and the merits of socialism.
b) Bill and Tipper jamming on the sax and drums while Hillary and Al boogie down.
c) A combined session with members of the Senate and the House of Representatives.

DEMOCRATIC PRO-CHOYS PLATFORM

Controversial!

5 small heads bok choy
¼ pound shrimp, peeled and deveined
1 teaspoon salt
1 teaspoon cornstarch
1 tablespoon cooked ham, minced
2 tablespoons vegetable oil
1 cup chicken stock
1 tablespoon cornstarch, dissolved in
   2 tablespoons water

   Wash bok choy. Remove outer leaves and discard. Separate the hearts of the bok choy into individual leaves; parboil. Remove and plunge into cold water. Cut each leaf in half. Place on platter.
   Chop shrimp; add ½ teaspoon of salt and 1 teaspoon of cornstarch. Divide this mixture evenly and place part on each piece of the bok choy; sprinkle the minced ham on top. Place platter on rack in steamer and steam for 6 minutes.
   In a saucepan, heat oil; add chicken stock, remaining ½ teaspoon salt and dissolved cornstarch. Stir until sauce thickens. Remove platter from steamer; drain off excess liquid; cover bok choy with sauce.

TERM-LIMIT TROUT

*Politicians, like fish, start to stink
when they hang around too long.*

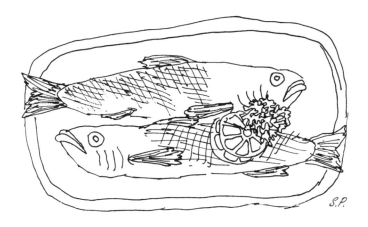

6 filets of trout
1 cup milk
1 teaspoon salt
¼ teaspoon black pepper

½ cup sifted flour
¼ cup butter
½ slivered almonds
Lemon wedges

Dip filets in milk, season with salt and pepper and roll in flour until entire filet is well-coated. Melt butter in skillet and cook fillets, browning evenly on both sides. Remove fish from pan to warm platter and keep hot. Add slivered almonds to pan; sauté. Generously sprinkle sautéed almonds over fish and serve with lemon wedge and parsley sprig garnish.

Discard Leftovers!

P.C.Q. #30

*Which United States
President had the shortest
term in office?*
a) James Garfield
b) William Henry Harrison
c) Grover Cleveland

★★★★★★★★★★★★★★★★★★★★★★★★★★★★★★★

BUN-CONTROL LEGISLATION

All the Bang without the Buns!

1 pound ground round
$2/3$ teaspoon salt
$1/4$ teaspoon pepper
1 — 8-ounce can tomato sauce
$1/8$ cup dry bread crumbs
$1/8$ teaspoon oregano
$1/8$ teaspoon basil
4 slices mozzarella cheese

Mix meat, salt, pepper, bread crumbs, oregano, basil and $1/2$ can of tomato sauce. Form into 4 patties. Brown on both sides in hot skillet; drain fat. Pour remaining tomato sauce over meat; top each pattie with a slice of cheese. Cover; simmer on medium-low heat for 10 minutes.

Add an Italian salad and a glass of red wine with lemon sherbet for dessert. A delicious light supper that won't show up on your buns!

★ ★

SENATOR ROBERT BYRD'S JURASSIC PORK

This one's been around for ages and it still tastes great!

1 — 6-pound pork loin roast
2 teaspoons black pepper
1 teaspoon salt
2 teaspoons white pepper
1 teaspoon cayenne pepper
1 teaspoon paprika
2 teaspoons thyme leaves
1 teaspoon dry mustard
4 tablespoons butter
2 tablespoons vegetable oil
1 cup chopped onion
1 cup chopped celery
2 cloves garlic, minced

Untie pork roast. Make 1-inch slits in top half of roast, about 2" apart. Place all remaining ingredients in a large skillet. Sauté 8 minutes; remove from heat; allow to cool. Place ¾ of mixture on bottom half of roast; cover with top half. Place remaining mixture in slits. Tie roast together with cotton string; insert meat thermometer into the roast. Place in heavy pan and cover with foil. Roast at 300° until thermometer indicates that pork is thoroughly cooked (at least 3 hours). Remove foil; turn oven up to 425° for an additional 20 minutes.

REPRESENTATIVE RICHARD GEPHARDT'S TAX AND SPEND SOUFFLE

The higher, the better!

½ cup butter
½ cup flour
2 cups milk
½ teaspoon salt
2 cups shredded Cheddar cheese
6 eggs, separated
1½ teaspoons dry mustard
Dash hot pepper sauce

P.C.Q. #31

V.A.T. refers to:
a) a large industrial container
b) Very Active Testosterone
c) Very Attractive Tootsie
d) Value Added Tax

Grease a 2 quart souffle dish; tie a double band of waxed paper around the top to form a collar. In a saucepan, melt butter over medium heat; stir in flour. Gradually add milk, stirring constantly until thick and smooth. Stir in salt and hot pepper sauce. Remove from heat and stir in shredded cheese until melted. Beat egg yolks until light; add to the cheese mixture. Stir in mustard and allow the entire mixture to cool completely. Beat egg whites until stiff peaks form. Gently fold the cooled cheese mixture into the stiff egg whites. Pour into prepared souffle dish.

Bake at 375° for 15 minutes. Reduce heat to 300° and bake for an additional 45 minutes. Serve immediately.

A classic!

SENATOR JIM SASSER'S DEFICIT $TEW

***In tough times
you have to cut back.***

1 pound lean ground beef
3 carrots, scraped and sliced
3 ribs celery, sliced
1 onion, thinly sliced in rings
1 green pepper, thinly sliced in rings
1 — 8-ounce can sliced mushrooms
¼ teaspoon basil
1 teaspoon salt
⅒ teaspoon pepper
1 can tomato soup

P.C.Q. #32

RIGO is:
a) A spaghetti sauce in a jar.
b) A famous Italian hairdresser.
c) Vice President Al Gore's
   plan for Re-Inventing
   Government.

Drain mushrooms, reserve liquid. Place half of the ground beef in a shallow greased casserole. Layer on half of the carrot slices, celery slices, onion and green pepper rings; sprinkle with half the seasonings. Cover with remaining ground beef; layer on remaining vegetables; sprinkle with remaining seasonings and top with sliced mushrooms. Combine reserved liquid from mushrooms with tomato soup and pour over all. Cover and bake at 350° for 1½ to 2 hours.

*Add southern biscuits, and a tossed salad;
serve ice cream sundaes for dessert.
A hearty and delicious family meal!*

GAS TAX BLUES

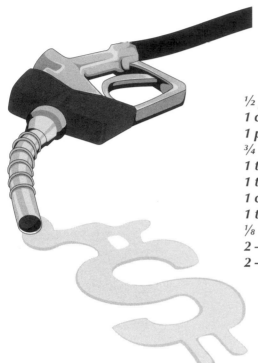

A real blow-out!

½ pound bacon
1 cup chopped onion
1 pound ground beef
¾ cup catsup
1 teaspoon salt
1 teaspoon dry mustard
1 cup brown sugar
1 tablespoon vinegar
⅛ teaspoon garlic powder
2 — 20-ounce cans baked beans
2 — 20-ounce cans kidney beans

Cut bacon into small pieces; fry until crisp. Drain on paper towel. Sauté onion in 1 tablespoon of bacon fat. Add ground beef; brown. Add catsup, salt, dry mustard, brown sugar, vinegar and garlic powder. Drain kidney beans. In a Dutch oven, combine beef mixture and all beans. Bake at 300° for 1 hour. Serves 10 to 12.

A great dish for tailgating before the big game —
if you can still afford the gasoline
to drive to the game!

Note: This recipe is currently undergoing
an environmental impact review.

REPRESENTATIVE DAN ROSTENKOWSKI'S GAME'S-UP DINNER

You gotta know when your goose is cooked!

1 wild goose, cleaned and washed
1 hell pepper, coarsely chopped
2 cloves garlic, sliced
1 large onion, halved
1 teaspoon salt
1/4 teaspoon red pepper

1/4 teaspoon black pepper
2 cups dry red wine
2 strips bacon
1 tablespoon flour
1 cup water
1/2 pound mushrooms, sliced

Pat cleaned goose dry with paper towels. With a sharp knife, make slit under each breast; fill with chopped pepper, onion and sliced garlic. Rub goose, inside and out, with salt and black and red pepper. Place some onion and green pepper inside the cavity of the goose. In a large skillet, fry the bacon; brown the goose on all sides in the hot bacon grease. Remove the goose from the frying pan and place it in a covered roaster. Add flour to fry pan, stirring until brown. Add about a cup of water; stir to make a smooth gravy. Pour gravy over goose. Place lid on roaster and roast goose at 325° for 3 to 5 hours, until meat is thoroughly cooked and tender. Add sliced mushrooms for the last 30 minutes of roasting time.

*Serve with a salad of oranges, apples and walnuts,
hot wild rice and fresh green beans — fabulous!*

SENATOR PATRICK LEAHY'S ST. PATTY'S DAY FEAST

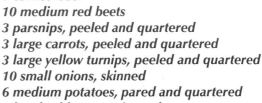

A cold bottle of Stout and warm soda bread with a chorus of "Danny Boy" make this a memorable celebration.

1 corned beef
10 medium red beets
3 parsnips, peeled and quartered
3 large carrots, peeled and quartered
3 large yellow turnips, peeled and quartered
10 small onions, skinned
6 medium potatoes, pared and quartered
1 head cabbage, cut in wedges
Fresh sprigs of parsley

Wash corned beef under running water; place in a heavy pot; cover with boiling water and simmer for 1 hour per pound. In a small saucepan cook beets in about a cup of water until tender; remove skins; set beets aside. When beef is tender, remove it from the pot and set aside. To the pot, add parsnips, turnips, carrots and simmer for 30 minutes. Add onions and potatoes; simmer 15 minutes. Add cabbage; simmer an additional 15 minutes. Add the meat; simmer just until meat is hot. To serve, place the meat on a large platter, surround it with the vegetables and garnish with parsley.

— Irish Soda Bread —

2 cups flour
1 teaspoon baking powder
½ teaspoon baking soda
3 tablespoons butter
¼ teaspoon salt
1 egg, beaten
¾ cup buttermilk
1 egg, beaten (to brush top)

In a medium bowl, combine flour, baking powder, baking soda, and salt. Cut in butter until mixture is crumbly. Combine 1 beaten egg and buttermilk; add to flour mixture, stirring just until moistened. On a floured surface, knead gently 10 times. Shape dough into a 6-inch round; place on a greased baking sheet. Cut a cross, ¼ inch deep, on top. Brush with 1 beaten egg. Bake at 375° for 35 minutes until golden brown. Place on wire rack to cool.

SENATOR DANIEL PATRICK MOYNIHAN'S LEFTOVER-BLARNEY SUPPER

*A **quick and delicious supper** for the day after the party!*

Leftovers from St. Patty's Day Feast on page 82
2 tablespoons vegetable oil

Chop leftover beets, cabbage, turnips, corned beef, onions, carrots and potatoes. Brown in a large skillet with 2 tablespoons oil. Cook until a light brown crust forms. Serve with baking powder biscuits and more cold ale for a quick and satisfying supper.

— Baking Powder Biscuits —
2 cups flour
4 teaspoons baking powder
1 teaspoon salt
2½ tablespoons solid shortening
¾ cup milk

Sift the dry ingredients together; cut in shortening. Make a "well" in the center of mixture and pour in milk. Stir until all of the flour is moistened. Immediately toss dough on a floured surface and knead 20 times. Roll-out to ½ inch thickness. With a floured cutter, cut rounds of dough; place on a baking sheet. Bake at 450° for 10 to 15 minutes. Makes 20 biscuits.

★ ★

SENATOR CAROL MOSELEY-BRAUN'S WELFARE REFORM

The Economically-Challenged deserve to live a little too!

4 — 5-ounce filet mignon steaks, frozen
½ pound fresh mushrooms, chopped
6 ounces dry red wine
4 tablespoons butter
Garlic pepper
Salt
2 packages refrigerated, prepared
 pie crusts (4 crusts)
2 eggs, beaten
Vegetable oil

Use lean, well-trimmed filets. Thaw for 25 minutes (steaks should still be frozen). Season filets with salt and garlic pepper; brush with a thin coating of vegetable oil. Sear in a hot skillet for 5 seconds on each side; place meat on a plate and chill. Remove pastries from package; unfold and set aside. Cook mushrooms in butter and red wine. Drain all liquid after mushrooms are cooked. Brush each pastry with beaten egg. Place 1 tablespoon cooked mushrooms in the center of each pastry circle. Place seared, chilled filet on each. Trim pastry so that there is just enough to wrap over filet , and seal. Place wrapped filets, seam-side down, on a baking sheet. Cut decorations from remaining pieces of pastry. Brush with beaten egg and place on top of each wrapped filet. Brush all pastry with beaten egg. Bake at 400° for 15 to 20 minutes for medium-rare, 25 minutes for medium steak.

SENATOR ERNEST HOLLINGS' TRUE GRITS

Fritz' Grits — A Southern staple with a bit of spice!

1½ cups grits
6 cups water
¾ cup butter
1 pound American cheese, grated
1 teaspoon salt
2 teaspoons savory salt
2 teaspoons hot pepper sauce
3 eggs, beaten
2 — 4-ounce cans green chilies,
    drained and chopped

In a medium saucepan, bring water to a boil. Cook grits until done. Add butter while grits are still hot. Add remaining ingredients in order given; mix well. Place in greased baking dish. Bake at 350° for 1 hour.

A nice accompaniment to grilled chicken or fish.

REPRESENTATIVE MAXINE WATERS' PEACE AND HOMINY

Let there be peace on Earth
and let it begin with U.N. troops!

2 cups hominy
1 can mushroom soup
½ teaspoon salt
1 teaspoon soy sauce
⅛ teaspoon red pepper
⅓ cup cornflake crumbs
1 tablespoon butter

Combine mushroom soup, soy sauce, salt and red pepper in a bowl. Stir in hominy; pour into buttered casserole. Sprinkle cornflake crumbs on top and dot with butter. Bake at 300° for 30 minutes.

'EARS TO YOU TOM FOLEY

A "must" side dish for any grilled meat!

½ cup butter, softened
¾ teaspoon salt
2 tablespoons chopped chives
2 tablespoons chopped parsley
Dash of pepper
8 ears of corn, husked and cleaned

Blend butter, salt, chives, parsley and pepper until well mixed. Spread 1 tablespoon of herbed butter on each ear of corn. Wrap each ear in heavy-duty aluminum foil. Place on hot grill, turning often, until tender – about 20 to 25 minutes. Serves 4 to 8.

SENATOR BEN NIGHTHORSE CAMPBELL'S FRUITS OF THE LAND

A tribute to Native Americans; a dish which beautifully celebrates the fruits of the land.

4 small acorn squash
1 cup chopped, cored apple
1 cup cranberries, chopped
¼ cup orange juice
½ cup brown sugar
2 tablespoons butter, melted

Cut squash in half, remove and discard seeds. Place squash, cut side down, in a large rectangular baking dish; add water to a depth of ½". Bake at 350° for about 40 minutes until squash is cooked and skins are still firm. Remove squash from pan, discard any remaining liquid. Return squash to pan, cut-side up. In a medium bowl, combine cranberries, apple, orange juice, brown sugar and butter. Fill each squash half with apple-cranberry mixture. Bake at 350° for 15 to 20 minutes.

Senator John Glenn's Out-of-this-World Buckeyes

A perennial Ohio favorite;
the rich taste will
send you into orbit.

½ pound butter, softened
1 pound smooth peanut butter
1½ pounds powdered sugar
1 — 12-ounce package semisweet
  chocolate chips
2 squares unsweetened chocolate

Mix together butter, peanut butter and powdered sugar until a stiff dough is formed. Roll into small balls and place on baking sheets in freezer for about an hour. Melt chocolate chips and unsweetened chocolate together in the top of a double boiler. Using a toothpick, dip each frozen peanut butter ball into the melted chocolate until almost covered. Leave a small circle of peanut butter showing and smooth out toothpick hole to make it look like a buckeye. Place "buckeyes" on wax paper-covered cookie sheets. Freeze for one hour, then store in airtight plastic bags in freezer. To serve, remove from freezer an hour before eating. Makes about 200.

SENATOR WENDELL FORD'S PRUNE WHIP

An Old Line Standard.

1½ *cups pitted prunes,*
    cooked and mashed
¼ *cup sugar*
1 *teaspoon lemon juice*
⅔ *cup whipping cream*
Pinch of salt

Whip cream until stiff. Combine sugar, salt and lemon juice; slowly add cooled prunes, fold in whipped cream. Chill. Serve with a garnish of whipped cream.

SENATOR HOWELL HEFLIN'S PRIDE OF THE SOUTH

A Southern Classic!

¼ *cup butter*
1¼ *cups brown sugar, firmly packed*
Dash of salt
¾ *cup dark corn syrup*
3 eggs, well beaten
1 cup pecan halves
1 teaspoon vanilla extract
1 unbaked 8" pie shell

Cream butter, brown sugar and salt until fluffy. Add corn syrup, eggs, pecans and vanilla. Mix well. Prick bottom and sides of pie shell with a fork. Place filling in pie shell. Bake at 350° degrees for 40 to 45 minutes. Serve with a generous mound of whipped cream and richly flavored coffee.

★★★★★★★★★★★★★★★★★★★★★★★★★★★★★★★

CAPITOL FILIBUSTER BARS

A great source of quick energy;
keeps you going during those marathon sessions.

2¾ *cups flour*
2¼ *cups light brown sugar*
½ *teaspoon salt*
2½ *teaspoons baking powder*
⅔ *cup butter*
3 *eggs*
1 *cup chopped peanuts*
1 — 12-ounce package
semisweet chocolate chips
½ *teaspoon vanilla extract*

Melt butter; pour into mixing bowl; add vanilla and brown sugar. Let cool. Add eggs, one at a time. Sift together flour, salt and baking powder. Add to butter mixture. Stir in chocolate chips and peanuts. Place mixture in a greased jelly roll pan. Bake at 350° for 40 minutes. Cool; cut into bars.

BI-PARTISAN-CHIP COOKIES

*An agreeable balance
that works together deliciously!*

2½ cups flour
1 teaspoon soda
1 teaspoon salt
1 cup butter
¾ cup brown sugar, firmly packed
¾ cup granulated sugar
1 teaspoon vanilla extract
2 eggs
6 ounces semisweet chocolate chips
6 ounces butterscotch morsels
¼ cup oatmeal

In a small bowl combine flour, baking soda and salt; set aside. In mixing bowl cream together butter, sugars, eggs and vanilla extract. Gradually add flour mixture. Stir in chocolate chips, butterscotch morsels and oatmeal. Drop by rounded teaspoonfuls onto ungreased cookie sheet. Bake at 375° for 10 minutes. Makes 3 dozen.

GERRYMANDARIN DELIGHT

*No matter how you cut it,
it's delicious!*

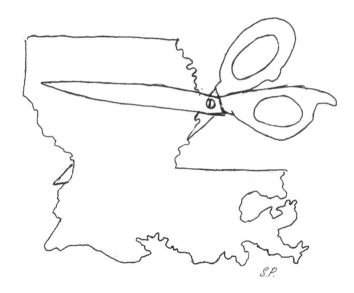

1 box butter recipe golden cake mix
1 stick butter, softened
1 — 11-ounce can Mandarin oranges, do not drain
4 eggs
8 ounces dry whipped topping mix
1 small box instant vanilla pudding
1 large can crushed pineapple, do not drain

In a mixer bowl, combine cake mix, butter, oranges and eggs; mix for 3 minutes at medium speed. Pour into greased, floured cake pan, 13"x 9"x 2". Bake at 350° for 35 to 40 minutes; cool completely. For frosting, combine topping mix, instant pudding and pineapple; refrigerate. Frost cake when completely cooled; refrigerate frosted cake.

CONGRESSIONAL PERKS

Keep warm while watching returns on a cold election night.

— Limousine Cappuccino —
6 tablespoons instant coffee
¾ cup whipped cream
3 cups boiling water
Cinnamon

Dissolve coffee in boiling water. Divide whipped cream evenly between 8 demitasse cups. Add a dash of cinnamon to each. Pour hot coffee over cream. Serves 8.

— Free-Travel Trinidad Coffee —
4 cups very strong coffee
1 teaspoon bitters slightly cooled
1 cup crushed ice
1 pint chocolate ice cream
Cinnamon sticks

Place coffee, ice cream, bitters and crushed ice in blender; blend for 1 minute. Serve garnished with cinnamon sticks.

— Expense Account Irish Coffee —
4 ounces Irish whiskey
6 cups fresh, hot coffee
6 teaspoons sugar
Can of ready to use whipped cream

Pour a jigger of whiskey in each of 4 tall mugs; add coffee, filling to within ½" of the top. Spritz whipped cream on top of each.

— Pay Raise Percolator Punch —
8 cups apple cider
2 cups sugar
4 cups cranberry juice
2 teaspoons whole allspice
2 cups orange juice
2 teaspoons whole cloves
1 cup lemon juice
6 cinnamon sticks

Pour cider and all juices into the percolator basket of a large coffer maker. Place the sugar, allspice, cloves and cinnamon sticks in the percolator basket. Turn coffee maker on and allow to perk through a full cycle. Makes 32 — 4-ounce servings.

HOUSE BANK HIGH-BOUNCERS

*Use fresh-picked June cherries —
the liqueur will be ready to
share at Christmastime.*

**1 quart fresh sour cherries, washed and pitted
1 cup granulated sugar
1 fifth bourbon or brandy**

Mix ingredients in a large container with a tight-fitting lid. Stir once a month for approximately 6 months. At the end of 6 months, strain cherries; pour liqueur into bottles. Store cherries, covered, in refrigerator to use as topping for ice cream.

"It could probably be shown that there is no distinctly native American criminal class except Congress."

— Mark Twain

In 1993 several individuals and issues hit the news because of their lack of political correctness. Even some of the Democratic Party faithful, anticipating jobs in the Clinton Administration, were left waiting in the wings.

The crossword puzzle below displays the names of some of these people who missed the boat. Test your knowledge by completing the puzzle; then enjoy cooking with those who Fowled-Out!

P.C.Q. #33 through #46

Across:

1. These people were canned by Clinton Aides and then reinstated after their firings became highly publicized.
3. CANDIDATE Clinton voiced his intention to accept refugees from this island nation. PRESIDENT Clinton decided against it.
5. Navy pilots belonging to this group held a convention during which several female fellow-officers were harassed and humiliated.
7. Former FBI chief, fired by Clinton and Reno, July '93.
9. Last name of the Interior Secretary who was reported to be the choice for Supreme Court Justice.

Down:

2. Name by which the fiasco involving #4 & #8 Down was known.
4. Clinton's 2nd unsuccessful pick for Attorney General.
6. Senator whose diary was subpoenaed for proof that he sexually harassed women in his office in the 1970's.
8. Clinton's 1st nominee for Attorney General; she withdrew after disclosure that she employed illegal aliens and neglected to pay Social Security taxes.
10. This former Wisconsin Congressman resigned from his Cabinet post in the Clinton Administration in December 1993.

12. This Democratic Governor's name was mentioned for a possible seat on the Supreme Court; he was not chosen.
14. This former Postmaster of the House of Representatives left his post after the scandal was uncovered there.
16. The first name of Clinton's longtime friend whom he tapped for Assistant Attorney General. Her controversial, liberal writings took her out of the running.
18. This perennial player in national Democratic Politics was not given a position of influence in the Clinton Administration.

CHAPTER FIVE
FOWLED OUT

CHICKEN À LANI GRUYERE

KIMBA WOOD'S WORKING MOMS ONE-DISH-DINNER

ZOË'S PERUVIAN CHICKEN

WHITE HOUSE TRAVEL STAFF'S BROKEN WINGS

WILLIAM ROTA'S GRILLED STOOL PIGEON

CHICKEN-JAM-SESSIONS

REVEREND JESSE JACKSON'S LEFTOVER-TURKEY DIVINE

BRUCE BABBITT'S FOILED AGAIN

BREYER'S YOGURT CHICKEN

SUPER MARIO SUPPER

HAITIAN-HOPES CHICKEN

SENATOR BOB PACKWOOD'S CHICKEN HARASSÉ

TAILHOOK TURKEY

LES'S ASPIC

Chicken À Lani Gruyere

S.P.

*Tender chicken, LIBERALLY
bathed in cheese.*

4 chicken breasts, boned and skinned
5 eggs, well beaten
¾ teaspoon salt
1 cup fine bread crumbs
1 stick butter
½ pound fresh mushrooms, sliced
6 ounces Gruyere cheese, shredded
1½ cups chicken broth

Cut chicken into strips. Combine beaten eggs with the salt; add chicken, set aside. After 30 minutes, roll chicken strips in bread crumbs; brown in butter. Place browned chicken in a casserole; add mushrooms. Layer cheese over mushrooms; pour chicken broth over all. Bake at 350° for 30 minutes.

Kimba Wood's Working Moms One Dish Dinner

*Put this together in a snap when you
get home from the office; while it's simmering you have
quality time to spend with the little ones!*

2 chicken breasts, cut in half
1 envelope onion soup mix
⅓ cup water
1 can whole tomatoes

Place chicken breasts in frying pan. Dissolve soup in water; add to pan; add tomatoes. Cover; simmer about 1 hour.

ZOË'S PERUVIAN CHICKEN

A marvelous recipe shared with me by a lovely couple who cared for my child.

1 — 5-pound roasting chicken, cut up
½ cup olive oil
1 large onion, chopped
1 green pepper chopped
2 cloves garlic, minced
1 quart tomatoes
Salt and pepper
1 small can tomato paste
½ cup chicken stock
2 bay leaves
2 cups uncooked rice
1 small can green peas
1 small can mushrooms
10 pitted ripe olives

Season chicken with salt and pepper. In a large skillet, fry chicken in olive oil until well browned on each side. Remove chicken; add onions, garlic and green pepper; cook until tender. Add tomatoes, tomato paste, chicken stock and bay leaves. Add chicken; cover; simmer 1 hour. Place rice in a saucepan and pour 2 cups boiling water into rice; let stand 15 minutes; drain. Rinse rice in cold water. In a medium skillet fry rice with 1 tablespoon of oil until rice begins to brown. Combine chicken and tomato mixture with rice and spread in a shallow roasting pan. Bake at 350° for 30 minutes, stirring every 10 minutes. Slice and sauté mushrooms; heat peas; slice black olives. Add these to chicken and rice just before serving. Serves 8.

THE WHITE HOUSE TRAVEL STAFF'S BROKEN WINGS

Pile 'em high and watch 'em fly!

2 dozen chicken wings
1 — 5-ounce bottle soy sauce
1 teaspoon hot mustard
4 tablespoons brown sugar
2 teaspoons garlic powder

Cut chicken wings in half, discard bony tips. Mix soy sauce, mustard, brown sugar and garlic powder in a shallow pan. Place wings in pan and turn to coat. Refrigerate for 3 hours. Bake at 325° for 1½ hours, basting often.

WILLIAM ROTA'S GRILLED STOOL PIGEON

This one's stamped first class!

6 pigeons, cleaned
Salt and pepper
6 strips bacon
¾ cup apricot preserves
2 tablespoons cider vinegar
2 tablespoons melted butter
1 tablespoon fresh ginger, finely chopped

In a small bowl combine apricot preserves, vinegar, melted butter and chopped ginger; set aside. Rub birds, inside and out, with salt and pepper. Wrap a slice of bacon around each bird. Grill over medium-high, direct heat for 15-25 minutes, turning once and basting with sauce for the last 10 minutes.

CHICKEN JAM-SESSIONS

Sweet and sour; flavor power!

1 fryer chicken, cut up
1 bottle red Russian dressing
6 ounces apricot jam
6 ounces pineapple jam
1 teaspoon dry mustard
2 drops hot pepper sauce

Place chicken pieces in baking pan. In a small bowl, mix together all remaining ingredients; pour over chicken. Bake at 350° for 1 hour.

For an informal get together add corn on the cob, sliced tomatoes and warm blueberry muffins — your guests will rave!

Rev. Jesse Jackson's Leftover-Turkey Divine

The answer for the turkey that's left hanging around in November.

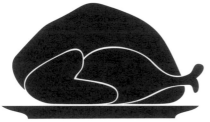

3-4 cups diced cooked turkey
1 package frozen broccoli spears,
    steamed just until tender
¼ cup butter
1 cup milk
1 can chicken broth
⅓ cup flour
⅛ teaspoon nutmeg
Black pepper
1 cup shredded cheddar cheese
½ cup shredded Swiss cheese
¼ cup grated Parmesan cheese
Paprika

Place steamed broccoli spears on bottom of baking dish. Place turkey on top of broccoli. In a saucepan, melt butter. Combine flour, nutmeg and a dash of pepper. Add to melted butter. Stir over low heat until thick and bubbly. Add milk and chicken broth. Continue to cook for 3 minutes on low heat. Mixture will bubble and thicken. Remove from heat; stir in Cheddar and Swiss cheese until melted. Pour sauce over broccoli and turkey. Top with Parmesan cheese and sprinkle with paprika.

Add cranberry relish and hot dinner rolls.
A praiseworthy meal!

Bruce Babbitt's Foiled Again!

Grazing Rights granted for these!

6 chicken breasts, split, boned and skinned
2 teaspoons minced parsley
1½ teaspoons minced basil
4 small shallots, minced
1 medium tomato, chopped
2 tablespoons lemon juice
2 tablespoons white wine
6 squares heavy foil 4" x 6"

Place 1 chicken breast on each piece of foil. Top with generous amounts of each of the remaining ingredients. Close foil tightly. Place in oven seam-side up. Bake at 350° for 35 minutes. These are great warm or cold.

With pasta salad, herbed bread and zesty lemon cookies, this makes an award-winning picnic.

Stephen Breyer's Yogurt Chicken

Tastes like you slaved; but oh so easy!

6 boneless, skinless chicken breasts
2 cups plain yogurt
¼ cup lemon juice
4 cloves garlic, crushed

¼ teaspoon salt
½ teaspoon pepper
½ teaspoon paprika
1 cup dry stuffing, finely crushed

Place chicken in a shallow dish. Mix together yogurt, lemon juice, garlic, salt, pepper and paprika; pour over chicken and refrigerate several hours or overnight. Remove chicken from marinade and roll in bread crumbs; place in baking dish. Bake at 350° for 1 hour. Serves 4.

SUPER MARIO SUPPER

Still waiting in Albany.

8 to 12 pieces chicken,
    boneless breasts and thighs
4 ounces olive oil
Salt and pepper
3 cloves garlic, quartered
2 green peppers, chunked
4 ounces fresh mushrooms, sliced
1 stick pepperoni, sliced
4 ounces New York State dry white wine
4 large tomatoes, cut in small wedges

In a large skillet brown chicken in 2 ounces of olive oil; add salt and pepper to taste. Sauté peppers and garlic in remaining olive oil. Add mushrooms and pepperoni to chicken; sauté. Add garlic, green peppers, wine and tomatoes. Cover and simmer 45 to 60 minutes until tender. Serve on a bed of steaming pasta.

*Pungent hot garlic bread and a crisp green salad
make this meal magnifico!*

HAITIAN-HOPES CHICKEN

When we land in America...!

1 — 5-pound stewing chicken
1 teaspoon salt
6 tablespoons butter
½ cup flour
1 cup milk
2 cups chicken broth
1 cup mayonnaise
1 teaspoon lemon juice
½ curry powder
2 cans asparagus tips

Wash chicken and place in pot of water; add salt; simmer about 1 hour or until tender. Reserve chicken broth. Remove meat from bones in large pieces. In a saucepan melt butter; blend in flour; gradually add milk and strained, reserved chicken broth. Cook over low heat until thick and smooth. Remove from heat. Add lemon juice and curry, mix well. Arrange 1 can of asparagus on the bottom of a rectangular baking dish; arrange chicken on top; pour sauce over all. Arrange the remaining can of asparagus on top. Bake at 400° for 20 minutes.

Serves a boatload!

SENATOR PACKWOOD'S CHICKEN HARASSÉ

Dear Diary... What a dish!

10 to 12 pieces chicken
    (Breasts and Legs are best!)
1 cup buttermilk combined with 1 beaten egg
1 cup flour
1 teaspoon garlic salt
½ teaspoon thyme
½ teaspoon black pepper
½ teaspoon parsley
1 teaspoons paprika
1 stick butter, melted

Mix flour, garlic salt, thyme, black pepper, parsley and paprika in a large plastic bag. Place buttermilk and beaten egg in small pan; dip each piece of chicken in mixture. Place chicken, 2 pieces at a time, in plastic bag, shake to coat. Place coated chicken in a baking dish. Drizzle melted butter over chicken. Bake at 350° for 1 hour.

Serve with mounds of fluffy mashed potatoes and fresh green beans.

TAILHOOK TURKEY

Take care with the gin, or this could get out of hand!

4 to 6 pound turkey breast
1 tablespoon curry powder
1 teaspoon thyme
1 teaspoon basil
¼ teaspoon garlic powder
1 tablespoon salt
1 teaspoon paprika
1 cup gin
1 cup water
1 medium onion, sliced
1 carrot, chopped
1 stalk celery, chopped
½ cup orange juice

Wash and pat dry turkey breast. In a small bowl, combine curry powder, thyme, basil, garlic powder, salt and paprika. Rub entire surface with combined seasonings. Place turkey and vegetables in an open roaster. Pour orange juice into pan. Place turkey in a 350° oven. Combine gin and water in a two-cup measure; use to baste turkey every 30 minutes. When gin/water mixture is used up, baste from pan drippings. Serves 8.

Serve this with wild rice in hollowed-orange cups,
cranberry relish and hot dinner rolls. Fit for the captain's table!

LES'S ASPIC

The less, the better!

1 can stewed tomatoes	¼ cup chopped onion
1 small box lemon jello	2 cups chopped, cooked chicken, chilled
⅔ cup boiling water	Lettuce leaves
½ cup chopped celery	Mayonnaise

Dissolve jello in boiling water. Add tomatoes, celery and onion; mix well. Pour into ring mold; chill for 6 to 24 hours. Unmold onto plate of lettuce leaves. Mound chicken in center of ring and serve with mayonnaise garnish.

Please note: This dish does not travel well.
Air-dropped over Bosnia, as a part of the humanitarian
aid effort, it made a real mess!

The United States Supreme Court is the highest court in the land. Charged with interpreting the constitution, the Supreme Court's deliberations and decisions become part of our American History. The nine Justices, nominated by the President, and approved by Congress, are appointed for life.

Test your Supreme Court PCQ. Fill-in the names in alphabetical order; then fill-up on their fabulous fare!

P.C.Q. #47 Justice_____

P.C.Q. #48 Justice_____

P.C.Q. #49 Justice_____

P.C.Q. #50 Justice_____

P.C.Q. #51 Chief Justice _____

P.C.Q. #52 Justice_____

P.C.Q. #53 Justice_____

P.C.Q. #54 Justice_____

P.C.Q. #55 Justice_____

CHAPTER SIX
AND JUSTICE FOR ALL

WILLIAM REHNQUIST'S ROBED WHEEL SUPREME

HARRY BLACKMUN'S BENCH-PRESSED CHICKEN SANDWICHES

"BACON" GINSBURGERS

ANTHONY KENNEDY'S STEAK-YOUR-CASE

SANDRA DAY O'CONNOR'S THOUSAND LEAVES TORTE

ANTONIN SCALIA'S MEATBALLS IN YOUR COURT

DAVID SOUTER'S ROE V. WEIGHT

JOHN PAUL STEVENS' FULL-DOCKET POCKETS

CLARENCE THOMAS' HABEAS PORCUS

WILLIAM REHNQUIST'S ROBED WHEEL SUPREME

Flawless presentation!

1 wheel Gouda cheese
1 package refrigerator crescent rolls
1 tablespoon spicy, prepared mustard
1 apple, cored and sliced into thin wedges

Open package of rolls; lay dough flat but do not separate. Roll dough into a circle about 1½" larger around than wheel of cheese. Spread dough with mustard. Remove wrap and waxy covering from cheese. Place cheese on dough; wrap dough up and around cheese. Press to seal. Turn over and place seam-side down on baking sheet. Bake at 350° for 20 to 30 minutes until golden brown. Dough should be crisp and flaky and cheese will be warm and soft. Place on serving plate; cut into wedges, surround with apple slices.

Enjoy!

★ ★

HARRY BLACKMUN'S BENCH-PRESSED CHICKEN SANDWICHES

Nothing trendy here;
just consistently good!

2 stewing chickens
15 saltine crackers, crushed
Salt and pepper
1 dozen sandwich buns

Cook chickens in covered pan at 300° until meat is very tender, about 1½ to 2 hours. Reserve broth. Remove meat from bones while still hot. In a food processor, grind the meat; add the cracker crumbs and enough reserved broth to make the chicken moist. Add salt and pepper to taste. Serve hot on warmed sandwich buns.

"BACON" GINSBURGERS

The turkey keeps it lean and kosher!

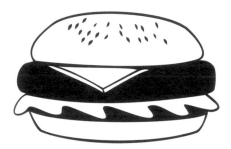

1½ pounds lean ground beef
8 strips turkey bacon
4 slices Cheddar cheese
4 whole-wheat hamburger buns, split
Kosher dill spears
¼ teaspoon black pepper

¼ teaspoon garlic powder
½ teaspoon onion salt
Fresh tomato slices
Lettuce leaves
Red onion slices

Fry or microwave turkey bacon until brown and crispy; set aside. With hands, mix ground beef, pepper, garlic powder, and onion salt. Form into 4 patties; grill on medium-hot grill to desired doneness.

Open hamburger buns; butter each half. Toast under broiler until lightly browned. When meat is almost done, place two strips of turkey bacon on each burger; top bacon with a slice of cheese; cover grill for 2-3 minutes.

Prepare serving plates with grilled hamburger buns, lettuce, sliced tomato, onion ring and pickle spear. When cheese is melted, remove hamburgers from grill, place on bottom half of bun. Serve open-faced with garnishes.

Enjoy!

ANTHONY KENNEDY'S STEAK-YOUR-CASE

Serious Steaks!

4 —1½" thick tenderloin steaks
1½ sticks butter
40 peppercorns
½ cup heavy cream
⅓ cup brandy, slightly warmed

In a 12" cast iron skillet, melt 1½ sticks butter; add peppercorns. Add steaks. Cook 4 to 6 minutes on each side. Transfer meat to a warm serving platter. Add cream to skillet; stir on high heat for 1 minute. Add warm brandy; light with a match. Remove from heat; pour over steaks and serve.

The ultimate in beefing!

Sandra Day O'Connor's Thousand Leaves Torte

No torte reform needed here!

2 cups flour
1 cup solid shortening
⅔ cup butter
4 tablespoons very cold water
2 packages vanilla pudding
3 cups coffee cream
2 tablespoons almond flavoring
½ pint whipped cream
½ cup walnuts, finely ground

Cut shortening into flour with a pastry cutter, or in a food processor. Stir in very cold water, just until dough forms a ball. Chill dough for 1 hour. Roll chilled pastry dough onto floured waxed paper. Cut out four circles of pastry each 8" in diameter. Place pastry circles on floured brown paper; prick each with a fork and sprinkle with sugar. Roll remaining pastry and cut out about 30 tiny elliptical leaves approximately ½" to ¾" long. Bake on paper, on a baking sheet, in 400° oven until leaves and circles are golden brown, about 8 to 10 minutes, watch carefully to keep from burning. Remove pastry, with paper, from baking sheet to a wire rack. When pastry has completely cooled, slide carefully from paper.

Make filling by preparing pudding according to package directions, substituting 3 cups coffee cream for milk. Stir in almond flavoring. Allow to cool. When cool, beat mixture until creamy and easy to spread. Place one circle of cooled pastry on footed cake stand; spread with filling. Alternate layers of pastry and filling, ending with filling. Frost entire torte with stiff whipped cream; top with ground walnuts. Decorate top with pastry leaves. Refrigerate until serving. Serves 10.

Serve with steaming coffee and
almond-flavored liqueur.

ANTONIN SCALIA'S MEATBALLS IN YOUR COURT

An entertaining favorite!

1½ pounds ground chuck
½ cup sour cream
1 teaspoon salt
¼ teaspoon pepper
½ teaspoon garlic powder
1 tablespoon butter
1 cup sour cream
¼ teaspoon garlic powder
½ teaspoon sugar
2 teaspoons dried dill
Paprika
Parsley

Thoroughly mix first 5 ingredients, mixture should be soft. Shape into small balls, about 3 dozen. Place on a tray and chill for 15 minutes. Heat butter in a large skillet; quickly brown meatballs; remove from skillet; place in baking dish and bake at 350° for 10 minutes. To the skillet add 1 cup sour cream; season with garlic powder, sugar and dill. Heat, stirring until just bubbly. Pour juices from baking pan into skillet and blend. Serve meatballs smothered in gravy and garnished with paprika and parsley.

DAVID SOUTER'S ROE V. WEIGHT

A scale-tipping choice!

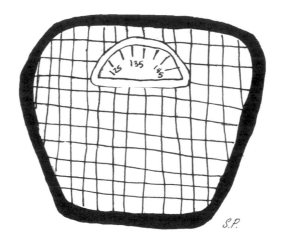

1 envelope unflavored gelatin
½ cup water
1 tablespoon lemon juice
1½ cups sour cream
8 ounces tinned red caviar

4 hard-cooked eggs, sieved
½ teaspoon salt
¼ teaspoon hot pepper sauce
1 tablespoon chopped chives

Sprinkle gelatin over water in a saucepan; place over low heat and stir 3 minutes, or until gelatin is dissolved.

Remove from heat. Stir in lemon juice, sour cream, caviar, sieved eggs, salt and hot pepper sauce. Blend in until caviar is broken up. Stir in chives. Turn into a decorative mold. Chill until firm. To serve, unmold on decorative platter. Serve with crisp wafer crackers.

Serves 6.

JOHN PAUL STEVENS' FULL-DOCKET POCKETS

A satisfying supper after a long day in court!

1½ pounds ground round
2 teaspoons dried parsley flakes
½ teaspoon oregano
½ teaspoon black pepper
¼ teaspoon garlic salt
2 tablespoons soy sauce

1 large tomato, chopped
1½ cups shredded lettuce
6 tablespoons sour cream
2 tablespoons horseradish sauce
12 Pita pocket bread halves
12 small slices cheese of any kind

Brown meat; drain. Add parsley, oregano, black pepper, garlic salt and soy sauce. Stir and heat thoroughly. Open pita "pockets;" place a small slice of cheese in each; place on a cookie sheet and heat at 350° for 5 minutes. While pockets are warming, combine tomato, lettuce, sour cream and horseradish sauce; stir into hot meat mixture. Spoon into warm pockets and serve immediately. Serve with cole slaw and fresh fruit for an easy and satisfying supper.

CLARENCE THOMAS' HABEAS PORCUS

Sumptuous fare for a Midsummer Night's Feast!

¼ cup soy sauce
¼ cup honey
¼ vegetable oil
3 tablespoons Dijon mustard
1 clove garlic, minced
3 scallions, chopped
2 pounds boneless pork, cut into 1" cubes
½ fresh pineapple

Combine soy sauce, honey, oil, mustard, garlic and scallions. Place cubed pork in a shallow pan; pour marinade over pork. Chill for at least 3 hours. Cut pineapple into 1" chunks. Alternate chilled, marinated pork and pineapple chunks on skewers. Grill until pork is thoroughly cooked, about 8 to 10 minutes per side. Serves 6.

Serve with hot, fluffy rice and a fresh fruit salad.

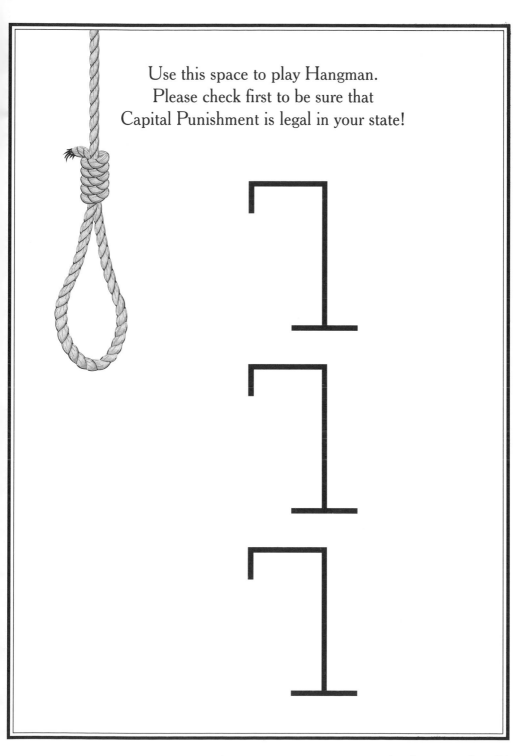

Use this space to play Hangman.
Please check first to be sure that
Capital Punishment is legal in your state!

Desert Shield, Desert Storm, Aid to Somalia, Tailhook Scandal, Gay Service Ban, Base Closings, Powell's Retirement...The 1990's have been a time of action and controversy, pride and turmoil, tradition and change.

Use the "military code" below to decipher the following 6 military buzz-words. Then turn the page and report for K.P. Duty!

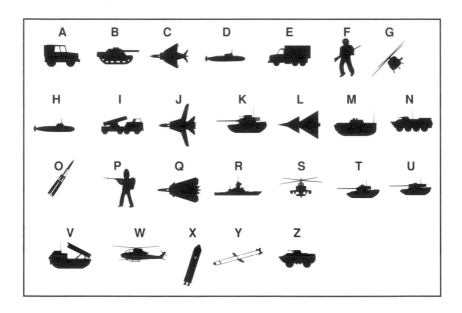

P.C.Q. #56:

P.C.Q. #57:

P.C.Q. #58:

P.C.Q. #59:

P.C.Q. #60:

P.C.Q. #61:

CHAPTER SEVEN
FROM OUR
ARMED FORCES

EGG MCBAGHDAD

S.P.U.D. MISSILES

COLD-WAR CHILI

NUCLEAR SUBS

G.I. JOES

CORPORAL PUNISHMENT

DON'T ASK / DON'T TELL C-RATIONS

SAILOR'S DELIGHT

BAR-NUNN

DESSERT STORM

NO-FLY ZONE

Egg McBaghdad

A *bit* of American ingenuity in a far-off land!

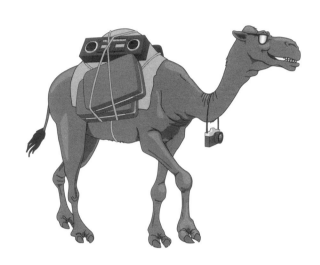

4 pieces pita pocket-bread
4 eggs, poached
8 strips crisp, hot bacon
4 slices American cheese

P.C.Q. #62

Desert Storm began with what on the night of January 16, 1991?

a) a food fight at the American Embassy in Kuwait

b) a nasty dust storm in the Sahara

c) air raids on Baghdad

Preheat oven to 375° while eggs and bacon are cooking. Place pita bread in oven to warm. Remove from oven and carefully open the pocket of each piece of pita bread and line the pocket with a slice of cheese and 2 strips of bacon. Carefully insert the poached egg. Immediately wrap in foil, seal, and place on baking sheet. Heat in oven 5 minutes, or until cheese melts.

S.P.U.D. MISSILES

These are a surefire hit!

4 large potatoes, baked until tender
1 tablespoon vegetable oil
½ cup chopped onion
½ cup chopped green pepper
2 tablespoons chili seasoning
1 cup cooked sausage, crumbled
1 clove garlic, crushed
2 cups shredded Cheddar cheese
1 cup shredded hot pepper cheese
1 cup tomato, diced
Sour cream for garnish

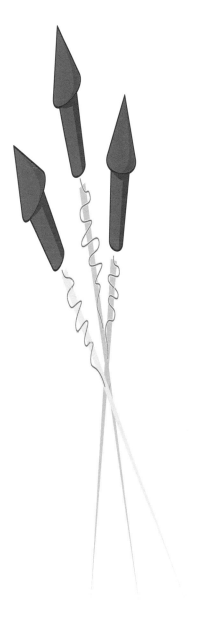

Cut baked potatoes in half while still hot; scoop out potato into medium bowl. Reserve shells. Mash potato with a fork to remove lumps. In a large skillet, heat oil; add onion, green pepper and garlic. Sauté 5 minutes. Add chili seasoning and sausage; stir well. Cook 3 minutes, then add potatoes, stir. Remove from heat. Stir in hot pepper cheese and 1 cup Cheddar cheese. Place potato shells on a baking sheet. Pile mixture into shells. Bake at 350° for 15 minutes. Serve piping hot, topped with extra shredded Cheddar and chopped tomato bits; offer sour cream on the side.

Add an avocado salad and finish with
lemon sherbet — a fun, casual dinner.

COLD-WAR CHILI

Not for the timid!

P.C.Q. #63

Which of the following President(s) served with distinction in the U.S. military?

a) U.S. Grant
b) Dwight D. Eisenhower
c) John F. Kennedy
d) Bill Clinton
e) George Washington
f) George Bush

2 pounds boneless chuck, cut into ½" cubes
1 — 19-ounce can kidney beans, drained
5 tablespoons chopped green chili peppers
1 envelope dry onion soup mix
1 8-ounce can tomato sauce
1 cup beer
2 tablespoons chili powder
1 — 10-ounce package corn bread mix
½ cup shredded cheddar cheese
½ cup shredded Monterey Jack cheese

Combine beef, beans and chili peppers in a 2-quart casserole. In a small bowl, stir together soup mix, tomato sauce, beer and chili powder; add mixture to casserole. Cover and bake at 350° for 1½ to 2 hours, until meat is tender. Prepare corn bread batter according to package directions; stir in shredded cheeses. Spoon batter evenly onto hot chili mixture. Continue baking, uncovered, for 25 to 30 minutes until golden brown.

Plenty of ice-cold beverages,
a tray of crisp raw veggies and
ice cream for dessert help to put out the fire!

NUCLEAR SUBS

4 large sub buns
12 slices mozzarella cheese
½ pound prosciutto ham
½ pound hard salami
1 ripe tomato, sliced
½ head iceberg lettuce,
    cleaned and shredded
4 ounces Italian dressing
Mild "banana pepper" rings

Split buns in half lengthwise; place on baking sheet. Lay slices of cheese on one half of open buns; place ham and salami on other halves of buns. Place baking sheet in oven on broiler rack; broil until cheese melts; watch carefully to avoid burning. Place lettuce, tomatoes, and pepper rings in medium bowl; sprinkle with Italian dressing.

Remove from oven and add lettuce, tomatoes and pepper rings on top of meat. Carefully close the buns; cut in half.

Serve with potato chips, carrot sticks,
and plenty of napkins!

G.I. JOES

Time-tested and true blue!

1 pound lean ground beef
1 large onion, chopped
1 green pepper, chopped
1 teaspoon salt
1 tablespoon sugar
2 tablespoons prepared mustard
¾ cup catsup
1 clove garlic, crushed
1 tablespoon sweet pickle juice
8 hamburger buns, split and lightly toasted
4 slices American cheese, cut in half
Dill pickle slices

In a large skillet, brown meat and add onions. Stir to brown. Add pepper, salt, sugar, mustard, catsup, garlic, and pickle juice; stir well. Simmer 30 minutes. Spoon meat over split buns, top with ½ slice American cheese and pickle slices.

Serve with a crisp relish tray, a basket of chips and icy watermelon wedges for a troop-pleasing patio party!

P.C.Q. #64

The government-issued can opener which comes with military mess kits is commonly referred to as:
a) a "one-armed bandit"
b) a "jackrabbit"
c) a "John Wayne"

CORPORAL PUNISHMENT

Breathe on enemies;
watch 'em drop in their tracks.

2 pounds lean ground beef
1 teaspoon hot pepper sauce
4 fresh Habañero peppers
6 Thai chile peppers
1 white onion, sliced
2 tablespoons butter
4 garlic buns, split and lightly toasted
4 slices pepperjack cheese
1 large tomato, sliced
4 leaves lettuce, washed and patted dry

Slice peppers and onions. **Caution**: protect hands with plastic or latex gloves. **Do not get any oil from the peppers in your eyes – it will burn!** Sauté peppers in butter. In a mixing bowl, combine hot pepper sauce and ground beef; form into 4 patties. Grill to desired doneness. Place a slice of cheese on each and cover until cheese melts. Place grilled burgers on bottom halves of toasted buns; place sautéed onions and peppers on top. Garnish with lettuce leaves and tomato slices.

Keep a pitcher of ice water within reach!

P.C.Q. #65

An M.R.E. is:
a) Maximum Restraint Environment
b) Materials Requisition Enforcer
c) Meal Ready to Eat. Government issued food for U.S. troops and for humanitarian aid

★★★★★★★★★★★★★★★★★★★★★★★★★★★★★★★★★★★★★★

DON'T ASK/DON'T TELL C-RATIONS

It's a mystery...

1 standard military issue field ration kit

Open kit. Remove 2 cans, 2 pouches, utensils and can opener. Open both cans. If they look like they should be mixed together, do so now. Don't ask, just eat them fast and try not to look at them while you're eating. Open 2 pouches. One of these should resemble a dessert; save it for last. Eat the contents of the other pouch, Don't Ask!

Reward yourself with the dessert. Pass the antacid!

SAILOR'S DELIGHT

Fabulous Fruits de Mer!

1 can peeled, chopped tomatoes
3 cloves garlic
8 ounces dry white wine
$1/2$ teaspoon basil
$1/2$ teaspoon thyme
$1/4$ cup olive oil
$1/2$ pound scallops
$1/2$ teaspoon salt
$1/2$ teaspoon pepper
1 pound Boston Scrod
$1/2$ pound shrimp, peeled and shelled
Fresh parsley

Sauté garlic in olive oil; add tomatoes, wine, basil, thyme, salt, and pepper; simmer 45 minutes. In separate pan, sauté seafood lightly with parsley. Place seafood in casserole and pour sauce over all.

BAR NUNN

Candy-coated and high powered!

22 single graham crackers, crushed
½ cup granulated sugar
½ cup melted butter
1 — 7-ounce package shredded coconut
1 — 12-ounce package semisweet
    chocolate chips, melted
1 cup dry roasted peanuts, chopped
1 can sweetened condensed milk

In a mixing bowl, combine graham cracker crumbs, sugar and butter; mix well. Press mixture onto the bottom of a 9"x13" baking pan. Bake at 350° for 5 minutes; cool. In the meantime, combine sweetened, condensed milk, coconut and chopped peanuts. Spread on top of cooled crumbs and bake 12-15 minutes; cool. Spread melted chocolate chips over cooled coconut. Allow to harden; cut into small bars. Refrigerate in airtight container.

P.C.Q. #66

"Shalikashvili" is:
a) a Hungarian dish made from chicken and red peppers.
b) a village in Eastern Poland.
c) General John Shalikashvili, Chairman of the Joint Chiefs of Staff of the Armed Forces.

P.C.Q. #67

"Semper Fidelis" is:
a) a line from the third verse of "O Come All Ye Faithful."
b) a rare form of canine distemper.
c) the motto of the U.S. Marine Corps "Always Faithful."

DESSERT STORM

Light up the night!

¾ cup firmly packed brown sugar
⅓ cup butter
6 ripe bananas, peeled and sliced
¾ cup rum
⅓ cup banana liqueur
12 scoops vanilla ice cream

In a skillet, melt butter and brown sugar; stir to keep from burning. Add bananas and cook until they just begin to soften. In a small saucepan, warm rum and banana liqueur for 1 minute. Place ice cream in 6 large, stemmed parfait glasses. Pour warm rum mixture over bananas; carefully light the top of the mixture. When flames die out, spoon bananas and sauce over ice cream; serve immediately.

When lit tableside, in a chafing dish, this is an elegant ending to a special dinner. Practice your technique before the big night to make sure that it comes off to perfection.

NO FLY ZONE

Shoe Fly! One sweet pie!!

1 unbaked pie shell	2 cups flour
1 cup molasses	½ cup brown sugar
1 teaspoon baking soda	¾ teaspoon baking powder
1 cup boiling water	⅓ cup shortening

In a medium bowl, combine molasses, baking soda and boiling water; mix well. Pour into unbaked pie shell. In another bowl, mix together flour, sugar, and baking powder; cut in shortening until mixture is crumbly. Pour over molasses filling. Bake at 350° for 45 minutes.

Cool and enjoy with a cup of Creole Coffee! How sweet it is!

Help the Vice President save the tree before the Lumberjack chops it down!

Set a timer for 30 seconds. Begin at the bottom of the tree, respond to each question. If you answer a question correctly, you move up the tree to the next question. If you answer incorrectly, then the lumberjack gets to chop down the tree! If you reach the top of the tree before the 30 seconds expires, Al saves the earth! If time runs out before you reach the top, you lose and so does the tree!

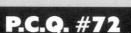

P.C.Q. #72

Which of the following creatures are on the endangered species list?
a) the white rhinoceros
b) the American bald eagle
c) the Buffalo
d) all of the above

P.C.Q. #71

Vice President Al Gore's best-selling book on environmental issues is entitled:
a) *Putting Planets First*
b) *My Life As a Tree*
c) *Is the Vice President an Endangered Species?*
d) *Earth in the Balance*

P.C.Q. #70

Translate the following titles to make them environmentally correct.
The Jungle Book to _____
Swamp Thing to _____
War of the Worlds to _____

P.C.Q. #69

What is an "Emission Control?"
a) A space-aged condom.
b) A device which attaches to the back end of a cow to reduce the emission of methane gas, thereby giving protection to the ozone layer.
c) A device which reduces the amount of pollutants that automobiles release into the environment.

P.C.Q. #68

What "3 R's" are taught to children in the 90's?
a) Readin', Ritin' and 'Rithmetic
b) Rockin', Rollin' and Rappin'
c) Reduce, Reuse and Recycle

CHAPTER EIGHT

EARTH LOVERS' DELIGHTS

AL GORE'S TOXIC WASTERS

TIPPER'S SKINNY-DIPPERS

MAGIC MUSHROOMS

CAROL BROWNER'S GREEN GODDESS SALAD

ONE MAN'S WEED...

GREEN, GLORIOUS GREEN!

GARDEN'S GLORY STIR-FRY

DOLPHIN-FREE TUNA LOAF

PRESTO PESTO!

ENDANGERED REESIES

OZONE LAYER CAKE

WHITEWATER RAPIDS

AL GORE'S TOXIC WASTERS

Mean and Green!

6 ounces vodka
6 ounces honeydew flavored liqueur
18 ounces orange juice
2 cups ice

Pour orange juice in blender; add vodka and liqueur. Fill with ice and blend well. Serve in a frosted stemware glass. Cools 4!

TIPPER'S SKINNY DIPPERS

Think Thin!

1 cup light mayonnaise
⅛ cup chili sauce
1 tablespoon white vinegar
1 teaspoon curry powder
¼ teaspoon salt substitute
½ teaspoon paprika
⅛ teaspoon ground black pepper

Combine all ingredients in a medium bowl; blend well. Cover and refrigerate. Prepare a plentiful assortment of fresh carrot and celery sticks, radish rosettes, green pepper strips, cleaned fresh mushrooms, broccoli, and cauliflower florets. To serve, place dip in a small bowl; place bowl onto a bit larger bowl of ice; place bowl in center of a large basket which has been lined with plastic wrap. Mound cold, crisp vegetables around dip in basket. Refrigerate leftovers immediately.

MAGIC MUSHROOMS

What a trip!

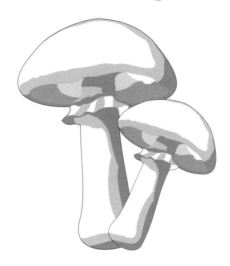

1 pound fresh mushrooms,
    cleaned and trimmed
¼ cup lemon juice
4 tablespoons olive oil
2 tablespoons sugar
3 cloves garlic, minced

½ teaspoon salt
½ teaspoon ground black pepper
½ teaspoon crushed oregano
¼ teaspoon dried thyme
1 can black olives, drained
1 red onion, sliced

In a small saucepan, combine lemon juice, olive oil, sugar, garlic, salt, pepper, oregano and thyme. Boil; reduce heat and simmer 7 minutes. In another pan, cook mushrooms in boiling water for 1 minute; drain and rinse with cold water.

In a medium bowl, combine mushrooms, olives and marinade. Cover tightly and refrigerate overnight. Add red onion just before serving cold, as an appetizer or antipasto.

CAROL BROWNER'S GREEN GODDESS SALAD

Earns the EPA Stamp of Approval.

Fresh salad greens, washed and trimmed
1 cup fresh parsley leaves, packed tightly
½ cup light mayonnaise
½ cup plain yogurt
2 green onions, finely sliced
2 tablespoons vinegar
2 anchovy filets, cut up
2 cloves garlic, minced
¼ teaspoon tarragon
4 tablespoons low-fat milk
1 clove garlic, peeled and halved

In the bowl of food processor, combine parsley, mayonnaise, yogurt, green onion, vinegar, anchovy fillets, garlic and tarragon; cover and process until smooth. Cover and refrigerate several hours. To serve, rub salad bowl with a cut clove of garlic; place greens in bowl. Stir milk into dressing mixture and toss with greens.

ONE MAN'S WEED...

Is another Man's dinner!

IMPORTANT: Use dandelions which have not been treated with fertilizers, pesticides, or other chemicals. If they come from a treated area or you are unsure of their source or treatment, do not eat them!

2 cups yellow dandelion blossoms
½ cup flour
½ teaspoon salt
¼ cup butter
¼ cup solid shortening
Salt water

Soak flowers in salt water for 30 minutes; drain well. Place flour and salt in plastic bag; shake flowers in bag. In a skillet, melt butter and shortening; add blossoms; fry slowly until just tender. Serve immediately.

GREEN, GLORIOUS, GREEN!

Adds zip to any meal!

3 — 10-ounce packages frozen spinach
3 tablespoons butter
⅛ teaspoon white pepper
¼ teaspoon salt
2 tablespoons flour
1 cup milk
9 ounces hot pepper cheese, chunked
½ cup bread crumbs
Parmesan cheese

Cook spinach in boiling water, until just tender. Drain well; place on paper towels and squeeze out excess water. In a small saucepan, melt butter; stir in flour and salt and pepper. Slowly add milk, stirring constantly, until smooth and thick. Add pepper cheese; stir to melt. Combine drained spinach and cheese sauce. Pour into buttered casserole; sprinkle with bread crumbs and Parmesan cheese. Bake at 350° for 30 minutes, until bubbly.

★ ★

GARDEN'S GLORY STIR-FRY

Who needs meat?

1 ½ teaspoons cornstarch
2 tablespoons cold water
2 tablespoons soy sauce
1 tablespoon sherry
2 teaspoons sugar
⅛ teaspoon pepper
¼ teaspoon garlic powder
1 cup fresh green beans, slant-sliced
1 cups broccoli florets
1 cup cauliflower florets
1 tablespoon vegetable oil
1 large onion, thinly cut in wedges
1 large carrot, peeled and slant-sliced
6 ounces fresh mushrooms, cleaned and quartered

In a screw top jar, combine cornstarch and cold water; add soy sauce, sherry, sugar and pepper; shake well and set aside. In a medium saucepan, blanch green beans in boiling water. Add cauliflower and broccoli; cover and simmer on low heat for 1 minute. Drain well.

Turn wok to high heat setting; add oil. Stir-fry onion and carrot for 2 minutes; remove and set aside. Add beans, cauliflower, broccoli and mushrooms. Stir-fry 3 minutes. Push vegetables up the side of the wok to remove them from direct heat.

Shake jar again and pour into center of wok. Cook, stirring constantly, until sauce is thickened and bubbly. Pull vegetables back into center of wok; cook 1 minute until heated through. Serve immediately with hot fluffy rice. Serves 4.

DOLPHIN-FREE TUNA LOAF

A favorite of Flipper's Fans!

2 cans dolphin-free tuna
1 can condensed cream of celery soup
1 cup fine, dry bread crumbs
2 eggs, slightly beaten
½ cup chopped onion
1 tablespoon lemon juice
1½ teaspoons curry powder

Drain dolphin-free tuna; save ¼ cup liquid. Flake dolphin-free tuna and thoroughly mix with reserved liquid and remaining ingredients. Pack into well-greased loaf pan. Bake at 375° for 1 hour. Cool in pan for 10 minutes; loosen from sides of pan and turn out onto platter. Allow to stand 5 minutes before cutting.

PRESTO PESTO!

Colorful and Delicious!

1 cup fresh basil leaves, packed
⅓ cup fresh parsley leaves, packed
½ cup grated fresh Parmesan cheese
¼ cup pine nuts
2 cloves garlic, sliced
¼ cup olive oil
¼ teaspoon salt
12 ounces fettucine

To make pesto, combine basil, parsley, Parmesan cheese, pine nuts, garlic and salt in bowl of food processor. Process, scraping bowl often, until a paste forms. Gradually add oil and process until blended. Cook fettucine according to package directions; drain and return to pan while still very hot. Add pesto sauce and toss with fettucine. Serves 10.

A loaf of bread, a jug of wine and WOW!

ENDANGERED REESIES

Grab 'em before they disappear!

4 squares unsweetened chocolate
2 sticks butter
4 eggs
2 cups sugar
1 teaspoon vanilla
1 cup sifted flour
¼ teaspoon salt
6 ounces peanut butter chips

In a small saucepan, melt chocolate with butter. In a large mixer bowl, beat eggs well; gradually add sugar, beating several minutes until fluffy. Stir in vanilla and chocolate mixture; fold in flour, salt and peanut butter chips. Stir well. Spray two 8 x 8 inch baking pans with nonstick cooking spray; divide batter evenly into pans. Bake at 350° for 25 minutes. Center should be fudgelike; do not overbake. Cool and cut into squares. Yum!

OZONE LAYER CAKE

Let the Sun Shine in!

1 box yellow cake mix
1 box instant lemon pudding
4 eggs
1 cup water
¾ cup butter, softened
For glaze:
2 cups powdered sugar
⅓ cup orange juice concentrate
1 teaspoon butter

Grease and flour a 13 x 9 inch pan. Combine cake mix, instant pudding, eggs, water and softened butter in a mixing bowl; beat for 4 minutes at medium speed. Pour batter into prepared pan. Bake at 325° for 60 minutes.

Combine powdered sugar, orange juice concentrate and butter in small pan. Boil until opaque. Pierce cake with a fork. Spread glaze over cake while still hot. Cool; cut into squares.

Enjoy with a scoop of lemon sherbet.
Don't forget your sunscreen!

WHITEWATER RAPIDS

Sure to be a wild ride!

EDITOR'S NOTE:

At press time, the "Whitewater" recipe file had not been turned over to the author. The Arkansas state trooper who was charged with making the delivery was called away on special assignment by President Clinton.

The White House reports its intention to make full disclosure soon.

P.C.Q. # 75

The Whitewater Development project was:

a) a federal project to maintain the nation's scenic waterways.

b) a Pennsylvania company offering white water rafting tours.

c) a failed Arkansas corporation in which Bill and Hillary Clinton were investors. Its demise fostered serious questions about the Clintons' financial dealings.

GLOSSARY OF COOKING TERMS

Baste – To pour liquid over food, particularly meat, while it is cooking.

Blanch – To dip food, usually vegetables or nuts, in boiling water for a brief amount of time.

Braise – To brown meat or vegetables in a small amount of fat, on the stove or in the oven. To commend.

Broil – To cook under direct heat.

Crisp – To cook foods until crisp. To soak vegetables in cold water until firm.

Cube – To cut into small, squared pieces.

Cut in – To blend, usually butter or shortening and flour, using two knives in a crosscutting fashion, or using a pastry blender. To ask someone else's date to dance.

Dredge – To apply a thin coating of flour crumbs, or seasonings. To search out old dirt on an opponent.

Fillet – To remove bones from meat or fish. A boneless cut.

Fold – To stir in with a gentle fold-over motion to preserve lightness. To go out of business eg: due to high taxes.

Julienne – To cut into small, narrow strips.

Mince – To cut or chop into very fine pieces. Candies to serve after dinner.

Pan Broil – To cook in a hot, dry pan.

Par Boil – To partially cook in boiling water or other liquid.

Pare – To remove the skin from fruits or vegetables by peeling with a small, sharp knife. Two of a kind.

Poach – To cook in a hot liquid just below the boiling point. To hunt without landowner's permission.

Puree – To produce a paste or thick liquid by processing in a blender, food processor, or pressing through a sieve.

Sauté – To cook in a small amount of butter, oil, or other fat, in a shallow pan.

Scald – To heat a liquid until hot, but not boiling. To yell at.

Score – To cut shallow, crosswise cuts diagonally in the surface of a meat with a sharp knife. To get points.

Steep – To let stand in a hot liquid just below the boiling point. Really high, eg: the tax on gasoline.

TABLE OF WEIGHTS AND MEASURES

1 tablespoon=3 teaspoons=½ ounce
2 tablespoons=⅛ cup=1 ounce
4 tablespoons=¼ cup=2 ounces
5⅓ tablespoons=⅓ cup
8 tablespoons=½ cup=4 ounces
12 tablespoons=¾ cup=6 ounces
16 tablespoons=1 cup=8 ounces
2 cups=1 pint=16 ounces
4 cups=1 quart=32 ounces
2 pints=1 quart
4 quarts=1 gallon
8 quarts=1 peck
4 pecks=1 bushel
16 ounces=1 pound
6 to 8 cups unsifted, all-purpose flour=2 pounds
3 to 4 cups sifted confectioners sugar=1 pound
2 ¼ to 2⅓ cups granulated sugar=1 pound
1 ounce by weight=2 tablespoons by measure

1 stick butter or margarine=½ cup
1 dash=less than ⅛ teaspoon
1 pinch=1 count sexual harassment
1 – 8-ounce can=about 1 cup
No.1 can=2 cups
No.2 can=2½ cups
No.3 can=4 cups
No.10 can=12 to 13 cups
1 teaspoon=5 milliliters
1 tablespoon=15 milliliters
1 cup=approximately ¼ liter
1 pint =.4732 liter
1 quart=.9463 liters
1 gallon=3.785 liters
1 bird in hand=2 birds in bush
6 of one=½ dozen of another
baker's dozen=13

INDEX

ANSWERS TO PCQ QUESTIONS

#1

Which of the following was not a Clinton campaign promise?

a) I will reverse the policy banning homosexuals from serving in the Armed Forces.

b) I will develop a National Healthcare System within the first 60 days of my administration.

c) I will not raise taxes on the middle class to pay for my programs.

d) I will keep a Kosher kitchen in the White House.

e) I will have a cabinet that looks like America.

f) <u>After I am elected I will not subject the American people to anymore news video footage of my jogging.</u>

g) <u>I will appoint my wife to act as co-president.</u>

#2 Seek and Find

#3

President Clinton's 1992 book detailing his philosophy of government is entitled:

a) Bigger Government; Better Government

b) <u>Putting People First</u>

c) Making People Pay

d) Making People Poor

#4

The film about Bill Clinton which was shown at the 1992 Democratic National Convention was entitled:

a) "The Man from Glad"

b) "The Man from U.N.C.L.E."

c) "The Man from La Mancha"

d) <u>"The Man from Hope"</u>

#5

The film in #4 was produced by which friend(s) of the Clintons:

a) Cecille B. De Mille

b) Steven Speilberg

c) Spike Lee

d) <u>Harry Thomason and Linda Bloodworth-Thomason</u>

#6

The correct spelling of the First Lady's name is:

Hillary _____ Clinton.

a) Rodman

b) Ramrod

c) <u>Rodham</u>

#7

Which of the following was a reason for Bill Clinton avoiding military service in Vietnam?

a) He didn't like the haircuts.

b) He got there late.

c) He disagreed with the policy banning homosexuals from service.

d) <u>It depends on when you asked him.</u>

#8

President Clinton has been known to enjoy playing:
a) the field
b) left field
c) around
d) <u>the saxophone</u>
e) all of the above

#9

Match the name of the person with the cost of their coiffure.
President Bill Clinton — $200.00
Hillary Rodham Clinton — $250.00
Ross Perot — $2.50
Al Gore — $15.00 cut, $20.00 lacquer
Lyle Lovett — 125 volts

#10

Who of the following Hollywood celebrities visited the President and First Lady at the White House during the first 125 days of the Clinton Administration?
a) Billy Crystal
b) Barbra Streisand
c) Sharon Stone
d) Richard Gere
e) Richard Dreyfuss
f) Paul Newman and JoAnn Woodward
g) Quincy Jones
h) Sinbad
i) Christopher Reeve
j) John Ritter
k) Sam Waterston
l) Hammer
m) Lindsay Wagner
n) Judy Collins
o) <u>all of the above</u>

#11

Among Bill Clinton's major goals are:
a) <u>promoting world peace</u>
b) seeking inner peace
c) getting a lil' piece
d) all of the above

#12

Hillary Rodham Clinton has served on the boards of which of the following corporations.
a) <u>Wal Mart</u>
b) K Mart
c) <u>T.C.B.Y.</u>
d) Y.O.Y.
e) <u>La Farge</u>
f) The Daughters of the American Revolution
g) <u>The Children's Defense Fund</u>

#13

Who of the following has not claimed to be Bill Clinton's half brother/sister?
a) Henry Leon Ritzenthaler
b) Sharon Elaine Pettijohn
c) <u>Ross Perot</u>
d) Roger Clinton
e) <u>Hillary Rodham Clinton</u>
f) <u>Rush Limbaugh</u>
g) <u>Joey Butafuoco</u>

#14

George Clinton was:
a) a used car salesman in Hope, Arkansas
b) a recently discovered half-brother to the President
c) the father of our country
d) <u>Vice President to President James Madison</u>

#15

Who was Leslie Lynch King?
President Gerald R. Ford's birth name. His mother changed it after remarrying when the future president was 2 years old.

#16

To what President is the following attributed? "You can fool some of the people some of the time, and some of the people all of the time, but you cannot fool all of the people all of the time."
a) Bill Clinton
b) Richard Nixon
c) <u>Abraham Lincoln</u>

#17
The Median Age of the Clinton White House Staff is:
a) 13
b) 21
c) 30 something
d) <u>42</u>

#18
Secretary of State Warren Christopher was:
a) dull
b) very dull
c) <u>very, very dull</u>

#19
Attorney General Janet Reno was:
a) a volunteer firefighter
b) a star of the Florida Gator Rodeo
c) <u>an accomplished Florida attorney</u>

#20
Agriculture Secretary Mike Espy was:
a) an Iowa corn farmer
b) an Arkansas hog farmer
c) <u>U.S. Congressman from Mississippi</u>

#21
Commerce Secretary Ron Brown was:
a) very wealthy
b) President of an international bank
c) <u>Chairman of the National Democratic Party</u>

#22
Labor Secretary Robert Reisch was:
a) Steward, Local 1560 UAW
b) a jockey at Saratoga Springs
c) <u>a Harvard professor</u>

#23
FEMA is:
a) the name of the human thigh bone.
b) a national women's rights organization.
c) <u>the Federal Emergency Management Administration.</u>

#24
Political Analysts and The Media dubbed 1992 the year of:
a) The chameleon
b) The Baboon
c) The Donkey
d) <u>The Woman</u>

#25
A Broad-Based Contribution is:
a) a charitable donation to a women's rights groups
b) a gift from the gals in the office
c) <u>a tax increase</u>

#26
NAFTA stands for:
a) a national chain of car parts stores.
b) "Now And Forever Aftah," part of Senator Ted Kennedy's wedding vows.
c) Vice President Al Gore's plan for reinventing government.
d) <u>North American Free Trade Agreement between Canada, Mexico and the U.S.</u>

#27
President Clinton's National Service Plan...
a) Guarantees affordable automobile maintenance for every truck, bus and car made in America
b) Mandates military service for cross-dressing trisexuals.
c) Provides discreet, inexpensive, illegal aliens to serve as Nannies to the children of wealthy attorneys.
d) <u>Provides tuition money to college students in exchange for service in national work programs.</u>

#28
The sign on Harry Truman's desk is reported to have read:
a) <u>"The buck stops here."</u>
b) "The bus stops here."
c) "The recession stops here."

#29

A joint session refers to :

a) Bill Clinton and his college pals rolling one and smoking, but not inhaling it, while discussing the evils of war in Vietnam and the merits of social-ism.

b) Bill and Tipper jamming on the sax and drums while Hillary and Al boogie down.

c) <u>A combined session with members of the Senate and the House of Representatives.</u>

#30

Which United States President had the short-est term in office?

a) James Garfield (shot after 4 months in office)

b) <u>William Henry Harrison caught a cold at his in-auguration ceremony and died of pneumonia 1 month later.</u>

c) Grover Cleveland (had 2 nonconsecutive 4 year terms)

#31

V.A.T. refers to:

a) a large industrial container

b) Very Active Testosterone

c) Very Attractive Tootsie

d) <u>Value Added Tax</u>

#32

RIGO is:

a) A spaghetti sauce in a jar

b) A famous Italian hairdresser

c) <u>Vice President Al Gore's plan for Re-Inventing Government</u>

#33 through #46

Answers to the Fowled-Out crossword puzzle on page 98.

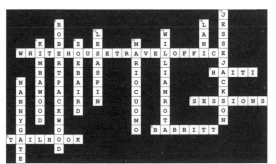

#47 Justice Harry Blackmun
#48 Justice Ruth Bader Ginsburg
#49 Justice Anthony Kennedy
#50 Justice Sandra Day O'Connor
#51 Chief Justice William Rehnquist
#52 Justice Antonin Scalia
#53 Justice John Paul Souter
#54 Justice David Stevens
#55 Justice Clarence Thomas

#56 ADID
#57 SOMALIA
#58 IRAQ
#59 HUSSEIN
#60 SCUD MISSILE
#61 TOMAHAWK

#62

Desert Storm began with what on the night of January 16, 1991?

a) a food fight at the American Embassy in Kuwait

b) a nasty dust storm in the Sahara

c) <u>air raids on Baghdad</u>

#63

Which of the following President(s) served with distinction in the U.S. military?

a) <u>U.S. Grant</u>

b) <u>Dwight D. Eisenhower</u>

c) <u>John F. Kennedy</u>

d) <u>Bill Clinton NOT!</u>

e) <u>George Washington</u>

f) <u>George Bush</u>

#64

The government-issued can opener which comes with military mess kits is commonly re-ferred to as:

a) a "one-armed bandit"

b) a "jackrabbit"

c) <u>a "John Wayne"</u>

#65

An M.R.E. is:

a) Maximum Restraint Environment

b) Materials Requisition Enforcer

c) <u>Meal Ready to Eat - government issued food for U.S. troops and for humanitarian aid</u>

153

#66
" Semper Fidelis" is:
a) a line from the third verse of "O Come All Ye Faithful"
b) a rare form of canine distemper.
c) <u>the motto of the U.S. Marine Corps "Always Faithful"</u>

#67
"Shalikashvili" is:
a) A Hungarian dish made from chicken and red peppers.
b) A village in Eastern Poland
c) <u>General John Shalikashvili, Chairman of the Joint Chiefs of Staff of the Armed Forces.</u>

#68
What "3 R's" are taught to children in the 90's?
a) Readin', Ritin' and 'Rithmetic
b) Rockin', Rollin' and Rappin'
c) <u>Reduce, Reuse and Recycle</u>

#69
What is and "Emission Control?"
a) A space-aged condom.
b) A device which attaches to the back end of a cow to reduces the emission of methane gas, thereby giving protection to the ozone layer.
c) <u>A device which reduces the amount of pollutants that automobiles release into the environment.</u>

#70
Translate the following titles to make them environmentally correct:
The Jungle Book to:
THE RAINFOREST CHRONICLES
Swamp Thing to:
WONDER OF THE WETLANDS
War of the Worlds to:
PLANETS IN CONFLICT

#71
Which of the following creatures are on the endangered species list?
a) <u>the white rhinoceros</u>
b) the American bald eagle
c) the Buffalo
d) all of the above

#72
Vice President Al Gore's best selling book on environmental issues is entitled:
a) Putting Planets First
b) My Life As a Tree
c) Is the Vice President an Endangered Species?
d) <u>Earth in the Balance</u>

#73
Among the President's favorite flowers are:
a) the Daisy
b) <u>the Rose</u>
c) the Gennifer
d) the Iris
e) the Black-eyed Susan
f) all of the above

#74
Which green vegetable has the First Lady reportedly denounced?
a) lima beans
b) spinach
c) <u>green peas</u>

75
The Whitewater Development project was:
a) a federal project to maintain the nation's scenic waterways.
b) a Pennsylvania company offering whitewater rafting tours.
c) <u>a failed Arkansas corporation in which Bill and Hillary Clinton were investors. Its demise fostered serious questions about the Clintons' financial dealings.</u>

Look for the
*POLITICALLY CORRECT COOKBOOK:
A KITCHEN GUIDE FOR THE 90'S*
in your local bookstore.

Or you may order directly from
the publisher by contacting:

WHITE PINES PRESS
P. O. BOX 472
GROVEPORT, OHIO 43125
1-800-913-3332